Rhythms of Grace

Worship and Faith Formation for Children and Families with Special Needs

by Audrey Scanlan and Linda Snyder

Cover Photographs: Leslie Jones

Cover Design: Christina Moore

Interior Illustrations: John Squier

Gathering Song: © 2008 Dennis Northway, composer

Trinity Prayer Cube photocopy master courtesy of Jenifer Gamber

Morehouse Education Resources

      a division of Church Publishing, Inc

Editorial Office: 600 Grant St. Suite 400, Denver, CO 80203

ISBN: 978-1-60674-055-2

TABLE OF CONTENTS

DEDICATION

We dedicate this book to our families who have supported us in our journey,
to John for his faithfulness,
and to Eli, a precious child of God and our best teacher.

To learn more about this unique and innovative approach to worship and faith formation,
or to connect with the founders of the program
visit
www.Rhythms-of-Grace.org

"Watch for the new thing I am going to do. It is happening already—you can see it now!
I will make a road through the wilderness and give you streams of water there."
Isaiah 43:19 (Good News Translation, Second Edition)

God's creative power touched us in the Winter of 2003 when one of our parishioners asked for help in negotiating church services with his six-year-old autistic son.

Eli had outgrown the church nursery and could not function without a full time aide in the church school classroom. Participating in the liturgy was difficult. In spite of the congregation's warm acceptance, Eli's father, John, felt uncomfortable and spent much of his worship time distracted and waiting for Eli's next outburst.

In an e-mail to the Rector, John explained his situation and asked for help.

God provided.

Rhythms of Grace held its first worship service in the spring of 2003. Combining storytelling, arts and crafts, therapeutic play and a celebration of Holy Communion, *Rhythms of Grace* was born as a new way to worship, strengthen skills, foster community, and be nourished at the Lord's table. At *Rhythms of Grace*, God had done a "new thing."

Create, with God, an even way in your wilderness... a river in your desert.
Celebrate God's great Rhythms of Grace.

WELCOME!

If you have ever struggled with the question of how to provide spiritual nurture and meaningful faith formation to children and families with "special needs," *Rhythms of Grace* may be just what you've been looking for.

By combining a sensitive, mindful and reverent celebration of the Holy Eucharist with a wealth of developmentally appropriate, experience-based activities, *Rhythms of Grace* takes a truly full-bodied approach to worship *and* faith formation—full-bodied in the sense of engaging children from the top of their heads to the tips of their toes; full-bodied in the sense of inviting lively and involved participation from each and every person, and full-bodied in the sense of welcoming the *whole community*—the *whole* Body of Christ.

If you are a parent of a child with special needs who is puzzled about how worship and faith formation fits into your lives, we offer the following: First, we understand that your child's spiritual development is important, regardless. We know its important to you, we believe its important to the whole community, and we have faith that its important to God.

Second, be assured that you are not alone. Having a child with a spectrum of needs that differs from many of their peers can be a potentially isolating experience, particularly as it relates to "going to church." But, that feeling of isolation doesn't mean there aren't others out there who share your experience or resonate with your particular situation.

Rhythms of Grace provides a way for all families to connect with a community of faith. At the same time, it provides an opportunity to share with others your faith practice and the many blessings and challenges that your child brings to your life.

In the pages that follow you'll find more information about how *Rhythms of Grace* works to meet the needs of children, families and communities. Then, you'll find a year's worth of monthly, scripture-based sessions (January through December) as well as 6 feast day sessions (All Saints', Nativity, Epiphany, Holy Week/Easter, Pentecost, Trinity). Finally, we've provided information on how to start and support a *Rhythms* program in your local community.

No matter how you've come to *Rhythms of Grace*, we hope that this resource provides a wealth of inspiration and suggests innovative ways for you to help God to do a "new thing" in your community of faith.

Our roots are in the Episcopal tradition, but all are welcome.

The Episcopal Church offers the gifts of an inclusive ethos paired with a careful regard for structure, dignity and ritual. Born in an Episcopal church, *Rhythms of Grace* is Anglican in nature but intended as wholly ecumenical.

There should be no doubt that *Rhythms of Grace* is a deeply Christian program—we regard Jesus as Savior and Lord, and following Christ's mandate in the Great Commission, we seek to "make disciples of all nations." (Matthew 29:19)

Rhythms of Grace has also always been overtly sacramental. We believe that in the nourishment of Christ's body and blood, we are renewed and receive spiritual grace to carry us forward. By virtue of the loving and inclusive nature of God and Jesus' work in the world, ours is an open table.

All who come are welcome to receive the sacrament and be strengthened in Christ. It is also possible to come, participate in the stories and activities and prayers and not receive communion. (Different faith traditions have varying understandings and expectations about the reception of Holy Communion and those guidelines are respected in our setting, and should be in yours.)

We honor differences through innovation and creativity, not labels.

Rhythms of Grace is a new response to caring for all of God's children. It is not a model that *mainstreams* children with special needs into an already existing program or worship service, nor is it a curriculum that separates and excludes.

It is, instead, a model that offers a variety of methods to explore God's holy Word, and appeals to many learning styles. *Rhythms of Grace* begins by acknowledging that many of us learn better with our hands, and that watching a dramatic presentation of a story or using story images is better for some than simply hearing a story read aloud. This means we may need to push at the bounds of traditional worship in making a "new way" in order to honor the sacred spirit in each and every person.

We are all created in God's image. With *Rhythms of Grace*, we do not focus on the special needs of individuals as *handicaps* or *disabilities*, but,

instead, celebrate the unique gifts that we all bring to the Body. We tell stories from Holy Scripture in ways that appeal to those with different core competencies.

Overall, our therapeutic play activities allow children to explore theological concepts in hands-on, practical ways that foster their social, physical, and spiritual development, and our celebration of Holy Eucharist is dignified but informal, allowing us to receive God's sacramental grace with deep comfort.

We serve children and families with a variety of needs.

While *Rhythms of Grace* was founded and designed to serve those with disorders on the Autism Spectrum, a number of children with different needs have come to worship with us, including children with Down's syndrome and other forms of mental retardation, neurological disorders, traumatic brain injuries, social and emotional deficits and motor disabilities.

All children—and adults—can benefit from an experience-based worship service, and in *Rhythms of Grace* you'll find that, in abundance. But, there are specific characteristics of various special needs diagnoses that may point you toward developing your program in one direction or another.

In general, of course, a broad-based program offering an array of choices is best as it shows the greatest degree of hospitality and meets the broadest spectrum of needs and interests. We would certainly invite you to customize your program to best meet the needs of those you intend to serve.

God's blessing on you as you pray and prepare to minister to these special children of God and their families, and venture into a new endeavor.

"...finally! A place where I feel comfortable in church!"

Karen, parent

Rhythms of Grace has the power to transform communities.

With *Rhythms of Grace* we experience what a blessing it is to open the church doors and say to everyone, "Welcome. Come inside. We have something for you."

Bringing *Rhythms of Grace* to your congregation will serve not only your local church, but the entire community of families with special needs in your area as well. It will be a blessing to those individuals and families and to the community as a whole.

Do not underestimate, however, the response of your own congregation as they, too, will be transformed. Some of this transformation will be joyful and come naturally as various gifts in various parishioners come to life. The Holy Spirit will manifest in wellsprings of generosity, acceptance and compassionate help.

Other parts of the transformation may at first seem more challenging and may require firm leadership to address anxiety, resolve conflict and chart the way forward.

At a minimum, as with any new endeavor, congregational life will need to shift to accommodate this "new thing." Here are the kinds of things you and your congregation can expect:
- Tables and chairs may be moved from their familiar places.
- Buckets of birdseed, sand, and corncob husks —used for sensory integration activities—will appear and be a source of curiosity.
- There may be resistance to a form of Holy Eucharist that is celebrated in a circle on the floor.
- There may be misconceptions, unspoken fear or anxiety, or general discomfort about how to welcome people with "special" needs.

But, this too, is what makes *Rhythms of Grace* a truly Christian endeavor—the opportunity and invitation to see Christ in everyone, no matter the resistance or preconceived notion. And, with the proper education and information, individuals and whole congregations can learn valuable lessons about ministering to the needs of others.

Rhythms of Grace is grounded in scripture, tradition and our Baptismal Covenant.

Jesus calls for us to care for each other and to give, lovingly. Our call as ministers of the Gospel is to offer spiritual nurture to all. *Rhythms of Grace* is a new way to extend Christ's hands in this world.

The New Testament mandate to *love one's neighbor as oneself* (Matthew 22:39), and Jesus' reminder that *just as you did it to the least of these...you did it to me* (Matthew 25:40), call for us to respond with compassion to those among us in need.

For families with exceptional children, the need is great. But, traditional liturgy does not often provide the room for spontaneity that families with special needs require. Conventional church school classes and faith-formation curricula are structured to accommodate "typical" children and rely on volunteer teachers who are not often trained or equipped to minister to a special population.

All of those who gather at a *Rhythms of Grace* service are part of the Body of Christ. Each time that we worship together, we create a new expression of that Body. At our services, the volunteers, musicians, parents, children and celebrant create, together, a place where Christ is present.

For those in traditional worship services, the same is true. Christ is made manifest in the readings, the prayers, four-part Anglican chant and the breaking of bread at the high altar. In *Rhythms of Grace* Christ is *also* made manifest through a felt board or water table, extemporaneous prayers, guitar songs with hand motions and the breaking of bread around a small wooden altar set on the floor.

Our Baptismal Covenant calls for us to "seek and serve Christ in all persons... and respect the dignity of every human being." (*BCP* p. 305) For families that include exceptional children, a *Rhythms of Grace* service offers respect in its effort to provide a form of liturgy that make sense to those who learn in different ways.

It is Christ's hand that kneads the play-dough, Christ's feet that teeter on the balance beam, Christ's voice that squeals with delight as a mountain of shaving cream is worked with the fingers.

THE BASICS

The cornerstones of the program: Storytelling, Therapeutic Play, Holy Communion

The format of *Rhythms of Grace* follows the same shape as a traditional service of Holy Eucharist, beginning with a celebration of the Word of God followed by Holy Communion. The Word of God is presented through a variety of methods that use visual cues as well as the spoken word.

The response to the Word includes engagement in different crafts, motor-skill development activities and therapeutic play.

Our rite of Holy Communion uses a simple prayer written for children that includes many of the traditional responses.

These three cornerstones: Storytelling, Therapeutic Play and Holy Communion are supported with Gathering Activities, Regathering Activities, a form for an Offertory Procession and a goodbye,—or Dismissal—ritual. These additional activities help with the transition from one major portion of the service to the next. The flow of the service is designed to allow for a worshipful time throughout, stressing joyful interaction with each other and the Spirit of God.

Planning: Amateur and Professional

Rhythms of Grace can be administered in any setting by a faithful corps of creative volunteers. Those with training in special education can certainly enhance the planning and implementation of the program.

The lesson plans that are included in this book have been created by a team of amateurs and professionals, among them, two special education

trainers, a Christian Formation specialist, a children's museum curriculum designer, a priest, a mother, a grandmother and a teenager. Each person on our planning team has valuable insights and ideas based on their experience and how they have encountered God's Word.

What is worship?

Evelyn Underhill has defined worship as "the response of the creature to the Eternal." And Graham Kendrick has described worship as "God's enjoyment of us, and our enjoyment of him." When we proclaim the Gospel in our services, we present the good news of God's love for us in Jesus and the rest is response.

The Word is the presence of the Eternal One among us, speaking to us in the stories of the Holy Bible. The response to God's Eternal Word may come in finger painting, tossing a beanbag in a basket or washing doll babies in a bath. The activities vary with the story, but the intention with which they are all completed is sacred.

Something deep and holy is evident at a *Rhythms of Grace* service from the opening moments when the children gather on the storytelling rug to the last beat of the Dismissal song: the gentleness with which the volunteers approach the children; the open give and take of quiet conversation between the parents; a sibling's helping hand; the joyful laughter of a child who splashes at a water table; the richness of the guitar strummed as the Eucharistic table is set; the raucous joining of voices in *Ev'ry time I feel the Spirit*; and the hush that comes as each child waits to receive the blessed bread.

There is no doubt that God is present, and we, God's creatures offer our praise.

The special needs network

In addition to the spiritual nurture received through the holy sacrament, the community, itself, at *Rhythms of Grace* is also food for the soul. Parents come and find time to talk with each other, pray together and worship in one place with their whole families present. Too many families with special needs children attend church at different times; often one parent stays home and cares for the exceptional child while the other parent attends services. Siblings are an important part of our *Rhythms of Grace* community and it is evident that they are relaxed in a setting where all are welcome. The special needs network is well connected, mostly through the internet, and many of the families who worship at *Rhythms of Grace* also know each other from school or play groups, therapeutic workshops or special events. It is a joy to be able to offer another place for these friendships to deepen- especially in the fellowship of Christ.

Prayer

The prayers that we pray at *Rhythms of Grace* come as we work and play. Christian prayer, our catechism tells us, is " ...response to God the Father, through Jesus Christ, in the power of the Holy Spirit." (*BCP* p. 856) Some of these prayers are extemporaneous, and others are more formal. The extemporaneous come, sometimes, in the form of discussion as we hear the Word of God.

In this informal setting, the children often ask questions or make comments about the story as we move along, and the Storyteller can help them to form their prayers. "What could you say to God about that?" We ask the child who, after hearing the story of the resurrection, wonders if her grandma is in heaven with God, too, and if she is, how come her mom is so sad?

Other extemporaneous prayers come in the form of games, asking children to name people or things that they pray for, or want God to hear about, as we roll a ball back and forth. The child who bows her head and says a quiet 'thank you' after receiving communion prays, as does the child who jumps up and down clapping her hands as the bread and wine come to her.

Formal prayers are part of the Eucharistic liturgy. Responses in the liturgy are prayers, as is the Lord's Prayer, said in each session at the conclusion of the Great Thanksgiving.

Body prayers are part of a *Rhythms of Grace* service. Some of the children have learned how to make the sign of the cross on their bodies and do so at appropriate moments in the liturgy. In using hand motions for the Lord's Prayer and sign language for some of our songs (sung prayer) we also pray and pay glory to God.

Time

Typically, A *Rhythms of Grace* service lasts between one and one and a half hours. We've found that a regularly scheduled mid-morning or early-afternoon time slot on any given Sunday is best for a *Rhythms of Grace* gathering.

The service should take place at a time when participants are rested and comfortable. Nap times and mealtimes—or the interruption of these critical events—can leave participants unable to focus and uncomfortable.

A variable time slot or the persistent need to reschedule can be disruptive to folks who benefit from consistency in both schedule and environment. A sponsoring church should be able to dedicate its time and space wholly to this program when it takes place. This communicates a level of respect and commitment to this ministry, and respects the need for consistency and the busy schedules of parents, participants and program volunteers.

Space

Ideally, the entire *Rhythms of Grace* service takes place in one large room so that participants can move freely from one activity to the next and still enjoy a sense of community. And, ideally the service should take place in the same physical location month to month.

In using the same space each time, returning participants engage in the activities more easily, and with less time required for acclimation.

The space should be safe. Wall outlets should be child-proofed, outside doors closed, bathrooms and kitchens kept secure. In a large room with several people working at different projects all at once, it is essential that basic safety precautions are taken.

"It's OK if my son just wants to watch. He knows that he is safe."

Kathy, parent

Organizing the Room

In planning and defining the physical space needed for the program, make allowance for the following:
- *Storytelling area*
- *Exploring Activity centers*
- *Altar area*
- *A Safe Space or Quiet Corner*

The *Storytelling area*, *Exploring-Activity centers*, *Altar area* and *Safe Space* should remain consistent from month to month, from gathering to gathering. Most facilities share space during the week with other groups; by retaining a consistent set-up plan, volunteers will be able to put the room together for *Rhythms of Grace* with ease.

It is also important that visual distractions be kept to a minimum during a *Rhythms of Grace* worship service. Remove toys, extra furniture, plants, books and other items before setting up for *Rhythms of Grace*. If it is impossible to remove these items, drape them with a sheet or drop cloth.

Sometimes it is helpful to have the Exploring Activity centers draped during the Gathering and Storytelling segments of the program in order that they don't prove distracting during the rest of the service.

With fewer visual distractions, the focus and emphasis will be on the activities designed to engage the congregation as they are happening.

Storytelling is best done with the children gathered on a rug around a felt board or another story prop to 'anchor' the area. Large beanbag pillows, rug squares or towels can be distributed to give each child a chance to create his or her own space within this common area.

A few folding chairs at the perimeter of the storytelling area can provide seating for parents and others who choose not to sit on the floor. These chairs can also help to define the edge of the storytelling space.

If the felt board is not needed, another 'anchor' can help to define the space. For example, in the telling of the Stilling of the Storm, the children could climb into a canoe or rubber raft. For the telling of the Nativity Story, a manger made from a refrigerator box might serve as a backdrop for the story.

Exploring Activity centers are set up at various locations around the room. Four or more activities are described for each session. Each activity should have its own space and volunteer to lead it.

Tables for Exploring activities should be the correct height to accommodate participants using chairs for mobility. In general, and out of safety considerations, activities involving large motor skills (mazes, obstacle courses, canvas labyrinth, rocking boats, bean bag tossing) need sufficient space.

Exploring Activities are to be conducted at their own particular tables. Carrying one unfinished project to the next table can become confusing.

The *Altar area* is used for the formal prayer and Holy Communion portion of the meeting. A small, low altar near the floor, around which participants can gather is ideal. A simple but dignified altar can be made from a small wooden crate draped with a beautiful piece of fabric.

While the altar and its elements provide the anchor, the cushions and rug squares used in storytelling can help to define seating space for the children during the celebration of Holy Communion. Adults gather on the floor with the children or in chairs, at the edge of the circle.

At each meeting a *Safe Space* or *Quiet Corner* is defined for those who may need to take a break from the activity. This space should be within view of the rest of the room, but marked as a space apart by the placement of a small rug or blanket. Comfortable cushions, stuffed animals and storybooks are good additions to this space. Children may opt to retreat to this space during the course of the meeting or to watch certain activities from the comfort and security of this part of the room.

In most churches, a fellowship or parish hall is an ideal space to accommodate a *Rhythms of Grace* meeting. Easily reached and fully accessible bathrooms and sinks are important. Tile or laminate counter top surfaces are optimal for craft projects, and area rugs can be rolled up and stored out of the way. If the church sanctuary is accessible, it may make sense to hold the Holy Communion portion of the meeting there. Sometimes the church space itself lends a different tone that is conducive to quiet prayer and can be very soothing.

Volunteers

The community gathered at *Rhythms of Grace* typically includes children with various special needs, their siblings, parents, grandparents, and caregivers, church volunteers, a Celebrant, musicians and others. But unlike other "special needs" programs that can isolate and exclude, the focus of *Rhythms of Grace* is on inclusion and community. All are welcome and all are nourished by this alternative model of worship and faith formation.

All come together to form a unique configuration of the Body of Christ, assembled for instruction, worship and praise. In the gathering, Christ is made known as we work, sing, pray and play together.

Specific roles for program volunteers include:
- *Facilitator*
- *Storyteller*
- *Activity Center Leaders*
- *Guides*
- *Celebrant*

The *Facilitator* keeps the flow of the session moving, from the Gathering all the way through to the Dismissal. The Facilitator helps new families become acclimated, notices which children need extra support, and assists the other volunteers as needed. The Facilitator acts as time-keeper moving the group in a timely fashion through the session.

Following the Gathering, the *Storyteller* assembles the community in a circle and shares the Bible story of the day. Stories are always told in a way that exceptional learners can understand, often including the use of props, story cards or other visual aides, spoken refrains or dramatic interpretation.

Activity Center Leaders organize and run the Exploration activities. Each Activity Center Leader stays at one center for the entire Exploration period assisting children as they come to each respective area.

Guides work one-on-one with children who may need more support than others, leading them through the centers, sitting with them at Holy Communion and assisting with transition times. Parents give Guides specific suggestions about how to best communicate with their child. When possible, it is a good idea for a Guide to work with the same child month to month.

In accordance with the canons of our church, the Priest or Bishop is the *Celebrant* who officiates at all celebrations of Holy Eucharist, including *Rhythms of Grace*. The sacramental portion of the service is designed to minister to the community and its varied needs while maintaining the dignity and order of Episcopal worship. (In establishing *Rhythms of Grace* in your setting, you will want to honor the guidelines specific to your denomination and your particular community of worship in selecting the Celebrant for your worship sessions.)

See Appendix II, page 137, for more on how to recruit, train and support volunteers.

Insuring Child Safety

Each local congregation should have rules and standards for creating safe spaces and insuring healthy experiences for children. This should include guidelines for screening paid staff and any volunteers involved in providing children's programming.

Remember to work closely with your church leadership to insure compliance with any and all policies, practices and procedures in place to safeguard children and families participating in your *Rhythms of Grace* worship program.

COMPONENTS OF THE SERVICE

Rhythms of Grace follows the form of conventional worship, but with important differences.

A *Rhythms of Grace* service follows the same sequence of events every time. This consistency in the pattern of worship allows returning participants to feel comfortable and to more easily make transitions. For each session, the sequence of events is Gathering, Storytelling, Exploring, Regathering, Eucharist, Prayer and Dismissal.

GATHERING (allow 15 minutes)

As participants arrive they are greeted by the Facilitator and if desired, invited to sign a guest book. The Facilitator may introduce members to each other and then explain the Gathering activity. One or more of the volunteers participates in the Gathering activity and encourages participants to join in.

The action of the Gathering activity is designed to be simple and engaging, allowing new members to join with one another as they arrive. Related to the theme of the day, this activity gives the staff and participants a way to connect right away, and gives the children an opportunity to become acclimated to the room.

This is also a time of gaining familiarity with the space. New faces, old friends and subtle environmental cues (a new rug, a ceiling fan turned on for the first time, or different lighting) may all be initially distracting and everyone may need time each month to get used to the space and to each other.

Gathering activities that use several areas of the room are ideal. For example, the children may color construction paper animals at a table near the door and then tape them onto an ark mural posted on a wall across the room near the Storytelling area.

Set aside a generous amount of time for the Gathering activity to allow for latecomers and those who may need more time to acclimate.

Transition Icons

Use the set of transition icons in Appendix I, (see pp. 93-98), to signal changes as your *Rhythms of Grace* worship service progresses. These icons help to orient newcomers and remind regular participants about what is coming next.

Worship Program

Provide copies of the Our Worship Service page found in each session to help orient participant families and help them choose the activities that most appeal to them.

SKILLS AND COMPETENCIES TARGETED IN EVERY RHYTHMS OF GRACE SESSION

Each session of *Rhythms of Grace* has been developed to include careful attention to a variety of specific skill areas or developmental competencies. The five target areas below are typically areas that are challenging for children with disorders on the Autism Spectrum, as well as children living with a variety of other neurological, developmental or social-emotional deficits.

The activities of a Rhythms session, particularly the Exploring activities, are designed to address and strengthen these various areas.

Fine Motor Skills

Examples: coloring with crayons, colored pencils or markers, stringing beads, tying and threading with yarn, sorting small objects, gluing various objects, painting, sewing, etc. The use of hand-over-hand instruction is helpful in some of these activities as a way to help children begin to master the specific skill required.

Gross Motor Skills

Examples: jumping on a trampoline, beating a drum, shaking a maraca, rolling or bouncing a ball, parachute play, following a path or playing hopscotch. Closely monitor the level of excitement or energy for gross motor activities, and help children return to a state of calm before moving on.

Communication

Examples: naming objects, asking for things, responding to questions, pointing to objects as they are named, giving and following oral directions, working together, and addressing others. Modeling good communication, having high expectations, setting clear boundaries, and providing meaningful reinforcement help build communication skills.

Tactile Defensiveness and Sensory Integration

Examples: searching for objects in buckets of dry rice, birdseed, husks, shredded wheat and other play media, free play in a water- or sand-table, planting activities with potting soil, etc. Be sure to communicate with parents about the tactile defensiveness needs of their child before proceeding with these kinds of activities.

Kinesthetic Awareness

Examples: shaking maracas, beating drums, tossing bean bags, walking a canvas labyrinth, walking on the balance beam, jumping on a mini trampoline, parachute play, negotiating a maze. Every part of every session presents an opportunity to engage the kinesthetic sense and foster an awareness of the body in space.

Storytelling (allow 10 minutes)

Telling the story gives the focus for the session's activities and allows for direct engagement with the Word of God. Items to have on hand for storytelling include a Bible, a Jesus doll, the story script, the story cards or other visual aides if any, felt board figures and/or any other props as needed. (Each session plan gives details as to what is needed for telling each story.)

Each story begins with the Storyteller showing a Bible to the group and announcing that the story of the day comes from the Bible, a special book that tells the story of God and God's people and God's son, Jesus. It is important to identify the story of the day as part of our Holy Scripture and to connect it with our faith heritage. Showing an actual Bible helps to make this connection.

The Jesus Doll

Each session of *Rhythms of Grace* makes use of and reference to a "Jesus doll." We use the physical presence of the Jesus doll as a tangible reminder of Jesus' presence among us in life and in worship. We find that the Jesus doll helps communicate a sense of both reverence and playfulness. The overall message is one of welcome: Jesus is welcomed here, and so is un-self conscious play.

(We recommend the Jesus doll available through Beulah Enterprises www.beulahenterprises.org).

With practice and experience, you may begin to explore a variety of storytelling techniques in order to convey God's Word in the most engaging way. In place of story cards provided with the session plan, you might use a felt board, story figures, dolls or stuffed animals to act out the plot of the story, or you might present a dramatic interpretation using costumes and props.

Some stories lend themselves well to simple repeated refrains as a way to maintain attention and engagement with the story.

In general, every story should have a visual component and use as few words as possible. Auditory processing is a challenge for many exceptional learners and attention to receptive language skills is important for many children on the Autism Spectrum, therefore, less is more.

Simply told stories, told slowly are best. Asking questions to check for content can be helpful, but it is important to allow ample time for responses. Children with auditory processing challenges need extra time to formulate answers and organize their thoughts. Silences are okay. The Storyteller should resist filling the silence with repeated questions or re-phrased questions. These can confuse children instead of helping them.

EXPLORING (allow 20-30 minutes)

This section of the *Rhythms of Grace* service allows for hands-on exploration of the story and themes of the day. Activities are designed to meet and address particular needs common to children with disorders on the Autism Spectrum and are intentionally "therapeutic." Typically, 4 different activities are planned for this segment of the program, and participants are invited to move through the various Exploring activity centers as their interest dictates.

The activities are chosen to relate to the theme or story of the day. Providing an assortment of activities that addresses a variety of learning modalities is important. For example, if the theme were the Nativity, participants might search for nativity figures in a bucket of straw, sort picture cards of shepherds and angels, have a corner to play with and care for baby dolls, or build a manger out of popsicle sticks.

Each of the Exploring Activity Centers is monitored by a program volunteer. Participants move to the center that interests them, or they are led to the activity by a Guide. If a child becomes over stimulated while participating in a given activity, some time in the Safe Corner might be appropriate, or a simple change in activities might help.

Sometimes a child will focus better on a small motor activity after some time in the gross motor area. Jumping on a trampoline, throwing a bean bag or moving through a maze can prepare a child to settle down for a quieter activity.

The Facilitator plays an important role during the Exploring time. Observing the play pattern of each child and their energy and interest level helps to determine when it is time to transition to the next segment. A series of verbal alerts that the next segment is due to begin ("5 minutes," "3 minutes," "1 minute") can be helpful, especially if the children are engrossed in what they are doing.

REGATHERING (allow 10 minutes)

The transition from self-directed play to community group prayer and participation in the celebration of Holy Communion can be a challenge. A large-group game or activity at this transition refocuses and regathers the group and prepares the community to continue in worship together.

For Regathering, the group comes together again in the storytelling area for a simple group game. Usually an adaptation of a game, like Red Rover, Red Rover or Simon Says, is ideal. At other times, simply rolling a ball back and forth calling children's names out loud is enough. Regathering activities for each session are described in the session plans.

At the conclusion of the game or activity, the Facilitator invites the participants to line up and move to the altar area.

In every session, the Regathering segment ends with the singing of *Jesu, Jesu*, which is Hymn # 602 in the Episcopal *Hymnal 1982*.

Participants then help by carrying some of the Eucharistic elements to the Celebrant or by leading the procession with a small cross. At the end of the procession, participants sit informally around the altar.

EUCHARIST (allow 15 minutes)

A simple Eucharistic prayer is used at each *Rhythms of Grace* service. The text of the prayer is found in Appendix I, page 100. Some of the traditional elements of the Great Thanksgiving are retained: The *Sursum Corda, Sanctus* and *Benedictus* and Fraction Anthem. Distribute copies of the Eucharistic prayer to those gathered for worship.

At each celebration, two children are selected to sit at the Celebrant's side and to assist at the Eucharistic table, holding the prayer sheet, elevating the elements and leading the congregation in the responses. Including the children in this way affirms their participation as ministers of the gospel and integral members of the worshiping community.

The Lord's Prayer is an important part of the Eucharistic celebration. In *Rhythms of Grace* it is prayed using hand motions. You will also find a master copy of the Lord's prayer with hand motions in Appendix I, on page 113.

> **Sharing Communion**
> Sharing communion at *Rhythms of Grace* is a blessing. Gathered together at the Lord's table, each person is fed and nourished in Christ's love. Children with special needs do not always understand the symbolism or subtle nature of the ritual and may express confusion or disgust, even, with the idea of taking Christ's body and blood. Good! This means that they are listening! Pausing to explain, briefly, the way that we understand Communion as a time when Jesus is made present is encouraged, but deep theological mysteries cannot be fully explained, briefly or otherwise to children *or* adults. Participation is the key. Extending one's hand and receiving Christ's deep love in a bit of pita bread is an enduring mystery and does not require explanation.

The Celebrant at the Holy Eucharist is always a priest or bishop, and if necessary, a licensed chalice minister assists in the distribution of Communion. The priest wears a stole and appropriate vessels and linens are used. The elements are grape juice and pita bread. The Rite II (*BCP*) words of administration are used: "the Body of Christ, the Bread of heaven, the blood of Christ, the cup of salvation."

Rhythms of Grace is meant to be an ecumenical gathering. Communion is an essential part of the program, but not all participants need to receive the sacrament. When greeting a new family, it is important to explain that during the service we offer Communion and all (the baptized) are welcome to receive. If a family feels uncomfortable about participating in Communion, they can be encouraged to participate in the prayers and to receive a blessing. (Note: It is always best to ask permission to touch someone before administering a blessing.)

> ### Go with the flow.
> While the structure and flow of the *Rhythms of Grace* service is important, it is equally essential to be flexible and open to individuals' moods and temperaments and to the particulars of the day. Did the program get a late start? Is the room excessively warm? Are there more participants than usual?
>
> It is likewise important to be open to the "stirrings of the Spirit." Some days are great days, and other days are not. Sometimes a group will connect with a particular story, offering responses, insights and questions, and other times there will be restlessness, lack of focus and multiple distractions.
>
> It may help to shorten the story if the group seems anxious. It may be beneficial to extend the activity time if everyone is happily engaged or moving through the stations at a slower pace.
>
> Worship is about resting in God, making a joyful noise, and communing with the Spirit and each other. Jesus moves though the gospels with gentle graciousness, with the zeal of one ignited by God, and with a tenderness that is healing balm. May we, as a community be similarly moved and responsive.

During this segment of the service, there is often a hushed and sacred feeling in the group. Intuitively, the children settle down and watch closely as the story of Jesus and God's love for us is told and the manual acts are performed. Small hands are outstretched to receive the bread and careful sips are taken from the cup as the Eucharistic ministers move through the assembled group. It is clear that the entire group understands that this is a holy time.

DISMISSAL (allow 5 minutes)
Music is an important element in a *Rhythms of Grace* service. *A cappella* singing or simple instrumental accompaniment is best. Use several favorite songs rotated at each gathering to allow participants to gain familiarity with the songs and participate more fully. Songs with simple hand motions, refrains or call-and-response formats work best.

Listening to instrumental music is also a good way to aid in transitions, particularly from the active engagement of the first part of the service to the quieter Communion portion. Playing music as the table is set and the congregation gets settled around the altar is especially appropriate. Also, playing recorded music during the distribution of Communion and immediately following helps to maintain the sacred time and space.

The children's hymn *Jesus Loves Me* is sung at the end of every *Rhythms of Grace* service as a post-communion hymn. In order to make the hymn an experiential, whole-body experience, and to facilitate communication where necessary, hand motion accompaniment is used in the refrain. See Appendix I, page 99, for a reproducible handout including the words to *Jesus Loves Me* and *Gather our Hearts*.

At the conclusion of the post-communion hymn, the Celebrant administers a blessing which the assembled participants receive by making the sign of the cross on themselves. The Celebrant then dismisses the those gathered saying, "Go in peace to love and serve the Lord." The participants respond, "Thanks be to God!"

THE SESSION PLANS

In sharing *Rhythms of Grace* in this format, we've designed the following 18 session plans to make them straightforward and easy to use in order to support the success of your programming efforts. Each session plan contains all the instruction you'll need for a successful session on the particular theme.

Each session plan is composed of four basic pages, explained below. In addition, some session plans make reference to other resources (story cards, psalm cards, prayer cards, templates, handout masters, etc.) You'll find these additional resources in Appendix I, starting on page 91.

The first page of each session is an administrative "at a glance" checklist of all the details that need to be taken care of before the session.
- The days scripture and theme, the time and date, and a list of the volunteers involved
- A list of all of the items you'll need for the days session activities in an outline form that parallels that day's session.
- A reminder for volunteers to come together at both the beginning and the end of the session to communicate with each other and to share a moment of prayer.

The second page of each session is intended as a "worship handout" photo-copy master for the session. This page summarizes the activities of the day, and lists for parents the specific functional areas targeted by each activity.

Make copies of this sheet (1 per family) and distribute at the beginning of each session. This worship program briefly summarizes the activities of the session and serves as a participant guide that helps everyone engage with the plan of the day. The icons for each section of the worship service correspond to transitional icon cards used within the session. Parents, participants and volunteers will appreciate this structured overview of the session's events, and will appreciate the attention to their child's needs that has gone into preparing the session.

The third page of each session is a detailed session plan that gives full descriptions of each activity, including what needs to be done ahead of time, what to provide participants and when, and the overall objective of each activity. Share copies of this page with your group of volunteers ahead of time, so that everyone is literally "on the same page" when it comes to conducting the session.

The fourth page is a Storytelling Script corresponding to the day's story. Here you'll find all the words you'll need to tell the story, and any further instructions to the Storyteller (*in italics*).

"I like Rhythms of Grace because it is the most fun I have ever had in church or doing anything religious."
Ben, age 10

"The activities and pace are just right ... and the format is flexible."
Jeff, parent

GETTING READY

The session plans on the following pages describe all of the items needed to conduct the activities of the session. Generally, these are common craft or household items commonly available at local craft or school supply vendors. We presume that you will have access to these kinds of materials well in advance of every session.

Occasionally, these items may take a little effort to find and obtain or create in advance of the session. We recommend that at the end of each month's session, attention is given to what is needed for the following month. That is the best way to avoid last minute surprises.

We've made some additional assumptions about the supplies you'll have on hand:

For craft activities, or for times when the activities might get messy, we assume you'll have ready access to the following so have not referenced them in each specific session plan:
- drop cloths, table coverings and smocks to protect clothing
- sponges, buckets, paper towels, mops, brooms, and dustpans
- ready access to running water.

BEFORE THE SESSION

The Transition Icons

In Appendix I, Support Resources for Year I, you'll find master copies of the transition icons for use in every session (see pp. 93-98). These images are on perforated pages so that you may remove them and make copies to suit the needs of your group. Since these images will be used repeatedly, we suggest making copies of these pages, either enlarged or original size, and mounting them on card stock or foam core. Retain the originals so that fresh copies can be made as needed.

Rhythms of Grace: Our Worship Service

The second page of each month's session materials is intended to serve as a participant handout—a kind of program of the day's activities. This helps parents, families and other participants orient themselves to the worship service, and prepare for what's coming next. Each month, make copies of this page for each family as part of your pre-session preparations.

Story Cards/Psalm Cards and Other Visual Aids

Many of the stories in Year 1 are supported with simple Story Card images or psalms, prayers or other text displayed visually. These resources are also found in Appendix 1 and are referenced directly by page number in their respective Session Plan. Before the session, remove these pages, make copies (enlargements or original size) and cut out the various items as directed.

The Song Sheet and the Eucharistic Prayer

Page 100 is a master copy of the Eucharistic Prayer used in every session. Page 99 is a master copy of the music for the Gathering song, and the words and accompanying motions for "Jesus Loves Me." Both of these songs are used in most sessions. Make a copies of these pages for participants in each worship service.

Rhythms of Grace • January Year 1

Theme: Jesus was baptized into God's Family.
We are baptized into God's family.

Scripture: The story of Jesus' baptism
(Matthew 3:13-17)

Date: _____

Location: _____

Volunteer Roles:

Facilitator _____

Storyteller _____

Celebrant _____

Center Leader _____

Guide _____

Items Needed for this Session

❏ **Gathering**
- ❏ assortment of small dolls
- ❏ church model made of foam core (Instructions in Appendix I, p. 101)

❏ **Storytelling**
- ❏ Bible, Jesus doll
- ❏ Storytelling Script
- ❏ large, long piece of blue cloth
- ❏ poster with these words "This is _____, a child of God, and in (him/her) I am well pleased."
- ❏ dove shape made of poster board

❏ **Exploring**

Baptismal Fonts
- ❏ water bowl, non-breakable, water
- ❏ a variety of small dolls
- ❏ jar of lip balm
- ❏ white towels

Water Table: Shells
- ❏ sea shells, assorted sizes and shapes
- ❏ water table or large plastic bin, water
- ❏ towels

People in the Church
- ❏ people shapes made from poster board
- ❏ crayons, markers or colored pencils

Doves
- ❏ dove shapes made of poster board
- ❏ white glue or glue stick
- ❏ feathers
- ❏ crayons, markers or colored pencils

Reenact Jesus' Baptism
- ❏ dove shape made of poster board
- ❏ large, long piece of blue cloth
- ❏ Jesus doll

❏ **Regathering**
- ❏ people shapes made from poster board
- ❏ mural-size kraft paper church outline
- ❏ elements for the Eucharistic table (see Eucharist)

❏ **Eucharist**
- ❏ altar table and elements (pita bread, juice, chalice, paten, purificator, corporal, altar cloth)
- ❏ Bible and Jesus doll
- ❏ Eucharistic Prayer (see p. 100)
- ❏ *Gather our Hearts* song lyrics (see p. 99)

❏ **Dismissal**
- ❏ *Jesus Loves Me* song lyrics (see p. 99)

❏ **Leaders and Aides Pre-service:** Set up space. Finalize details. Pray.
❏ **Leaders and Aides Post-service:** Clean-up and share feedback. Set dates, discuss theme for next month.

Rhythms of Grace

Today's Theme:	Jesus was baptized into God's Family. We are baptized into God's family.
Today's Scripture:	The story of Jesus' baptism (Matthew 3:13-17)

Our Worship Service

Gathering

We symbolize gathering together as a Christian family by finding representations of ourselves and bringing them together in a model of the church.

Storytelling

Today we hear the story of Jesus' baptism in the Jordan river.

Exploring

Baptismal Fonts
Explore the ritual of Baptism, practice pouring the water and sealing with oil.
(*sensory integration, gross motor, communication*)

Water Table: Shells
Experiment with seashells and water.
(*gross motor, sensory integration*)

People in the Church
Create self-portraits to display together on a Church mural.
(*fine motor, communication*)

Doves
Create and decorate poster board cut-outs of doves.
(*fine motor, communication*)

Reenact Jesus' Baptism
Engage in free play reenacting the story of Jesus' baptism.
(*gross motor, sensory integration, kinesthetic awareness*)

Regathering

We show ourselves as part of the Body of Christ by placing representations of ourselves inside the church.
Sing *Jesu, Jesu.*
We bring elements of the Eucharist to the Celebrant to create the Eucharistic table.

Eucharist

Sing: *Gather our Hearts*
Gather our hearts, oh God.
Gather our thoughts, oh God.
Bring us together around you.

Celebration of the Eucharist

Dismissal

Sing and Sign: *Jesus Loves Me*
Blessing
Celebrant: "Go in Peace to Love and Serve the Lord."
Participants: "Thanks be to God!"

This Month's Session Plan

Gathering

Before the session, create the church model from foam core according to the instructions (Appendix I, p. 101). Hide an assortment of small dolls around the worship space. Place church model in the middle of the room.
Together children and adults find the dolls and place them in the model church.

Storytelling

Theme: Jesus was baptized into God's Family. We are baptized into God's family.
Before the session, create poster with "This is _____, a child of God, and in (him/her) I am well pleased." Place blue cloth on the floor to represent a river.
Hang poster board dove shape above storytelling area.
See Storytelling Script on following page.
Place the Bible and the Jesus doll by the Storyteller.

Exploring

Baptismal Fonts
Create a font using a large, non-breakable bowl. Reenact the story, or have leader show how babies are baptized using dolls, a shell to pour the water, and a small container of lip balm to "seal" baby's forehead with a cross.

Water Table: Shells
Place a variety of shells in a water table for imaginative water play.

People in the Church
Participants color/design a self-portrait from the cut-outs of people. (Save to use later in Regathering.)

Doves
Participants color and glue feathers onto poster board cut-outs of doves.

Reenact Jesus' Baptism
Using the Jesus doll or themselves, invite children to use blue "river" cloth and dove shape from Storytelling to play act Jesus' baptism.

Regathering

Call each participant by name to place themselves—the cut-outs from People in the Church (see above)—on the church outline hung on the wall.
Singing *Jesu, Jesu* participants bring Eucharistic elements to the Celebrant then sit in a circle around the Eucharistic table.

Eucharist

Sing: *Gather our Hearts*
Gather our hearts, oh God.
Gather our thoughts, oh God.
Bring us together around you.

Celebration of the Eucharist

Dismissal

All sing and sign *Jesus Loves Me*.
Celebrant provides the blessing:
Celebrant: "Go in Peace to Love and Serve the Lord."
Participants: "Thanks be to God!"

storytelling Script

Our story today is from our Bible (*show Bible*), our book that tells the stories of God and God's people, of Jesus (*show Jesus doll*), God's son, and of how much God loves us (*place hands over heart*).

Today's story is from the second part of our Bible.

Show Bible and divide it in half by placing your hand between the left and right halves.

The second part of our Bible is called the New Testament. It has the stories of Jesus.

When Jesus was a young man and ready to begin his ministry, he traveled to the place where his cousin, John the Baptist, was baptizing people in the Jordan River. People were baptized as a way to ask God's forgiveness and to begin again.

When Jesus saw John he went into the water and asked John to baptize him.

Jesus went down into the water. As he rose back out of the water, the sky opened, a dove appeared (*point to the dove, above*) and God spoke, "This is my son and in him I am well pleased."

Jesus left the river and went into the desert to be alone with God and to pray.

We are baptized with water when we join God's family. Let's all pretend to be baptized.

Invite parents to help baptize each child. Using words from the story and the child's name, enact a pretend baptism. Demonstrate by baptizing the Jesus doll. Refer to the poster with these words:

"This is (*insert child's name*) a child of God, and in (*him/her*) I am well pleased."

Amen.

After an appropriate pause, the Storyteller goes on to explain the activities of the day.

Rhythms of Grace • February Year 1

Theme: Jesus invites us to enter the Kingdom of God.

Scripture: The Hidden Treasure (Matthew 13:44)
The Pearl of Great Value (Matthew 13:45)

Date: _____

Location: _____

Volunteer Roles:

Facilitator _____

Storyteller _____

Celebrant _____

Center Leader _____

Guide _____

Items Needed for this Session

❑ **Gathering**
- ❑ gold coins
- ❑ wooden box/treasure chest

❑ **Storytelling**
- ❑ Bible, Jesus doll
- ❑ Storytelling Script
- ❑ gold coins, wooden box/treasure chest
- ❑ plastic pearls of various sizes and colors
- ❑ large styrofoam ball (large pearl)

❑ **Exploring**

Pearl Stringing
- ❑ plastic pearls of various sizes and colors
- ❑ wire, string, yarn, floss
- ❑ scissors

Coin Search
- ❑ gold coins
- ❑ large bucket
- ❑ packing peanuts, dry rice or sterilized potting soil

Collage
- ❑ poster board with treasure chest drawn on it
- ❑ magazine photos of "treasure" items
- ❑ white glue or glue sticks

Treasure Box Painting
- ❑ small wooden boxes
- ❑ craft paints, brushes, water

Treasure Hunt Path
- ❑ 8 ½" x 11" foam squares in various colors
- ❑ treasure chest and coins from Gathering and Storytelling

❑ **Regathering**
- ❑ large styrofoam ball (from Storytelling)
- ❑ recorded music, player
- ❑ elements for the Eucharistic table (see Eucharist)

❑ **Eucharist**
- ❑ altar table and elements (pita bread, juice, chalice, paten, purificator, corporal, altar cloth)
- ❑ Bible and Jesus doll
- ❑ Eucharistic Prayer (see p. 100)
- ❑ *Gather our Hearts* song lyrics (see p. 99)

❑ **Dismissal**
- ❑ *Jesus Loves Me* song lyrics (see p. 99)

❑ **Leaders and Aides Pre-service:** Set up space. Finalize details. Pray.
❑ **Leaders and Aides Post-service:** Clean-up and share feedback. Set dates, discuss theme for next month.

Rhythms of Grace

Today's Theme:	Jesus invites us to enter the Kingdom of God.
Today's Scripture:	The Hidden Treasure (Matthew 13:44) and The Pearl of Great Value (Matthew 13:45)

Our Worship Service

Gathering

We begin to call to mind the notion of treasure—used in this session's parables as a metaphor for understanding the Kingdom of God—by gathering together hidden gold coins.

Storytelling

Today we hear two stories about the Kingdom of Heaven: The Parable of the Hidden Treasure, and the Parable of the Great Pearl.

Exploring

Pearl Stringing
Children make and share their own string-of-pearls craft.
(*fine motor, sensory integration*)

Coin Search
Participants search for buried treasure.
(*gross motor, sensory integration*)

Collage
Children explore the idea of treasure with a collage activity.
(*communication, fine motor*)

Treasure Box Painting
Children create their own colorful treasure box to take home.
(*fine motor, communication*)

Treasure Hunt Path
Participants follow the path and receive the treasure.
(*gross motor, kinesthetic awareness*)

Regathering

Play Pass-the-Pearl to affirm that we are all treasured in the Kingdom of God.
Sing *Jesu, Jesu*.
We bring elements of the Eucharist to the Celebrant to create the Eucharistic table.

Eucharist

Sing: *Gather our Hearts*
Gather our hearts, oh God.
Gather our thoughts, oh God.
Bring us together around you.

Celebration of the Eucharist

Dismissal

Sing and Sign: *Jesus Loves Me*
Blessing
Celebrant: "Go in Peace to Love and Serve the Lord."
Participants: "Thanks be to God!"

This Month's Session Plan

Gathering	Before the session, hide gold coins in various locations around the room. Place the treasure chest in a prominent location, visible to all as they arrive. As participants arrive, they are invited to gather gold coins hidden around the room and put them in the treasure chest.
Storytelling	Theme: Jesus invites us to enter the Kingdom of God. See Storytelling Script on the following page. Place the Bible and the Jesus doll by the Storyteller. Place the treasure chest with gold coins and the assortment of pearl-shaped beads hidden from view but within reach of the Storyteller. Keep the large pearl hidden until the last as indicated in the story text.

Exploring

Pearl Stringing
Children string colored pearls (beads) of various sizes on strings of various widths, knotted on one end. Provide larger beads with large holes and thicker string or yarn, as well as small beads, beading wire or floss.

Coin Search
Children search for "treasure" (gold coins from the Gathering activity) buried in a giant pot or bin of sterilized potting soil. Children sift through material to find coins.

Collage
On large poster board, draw an image of a treasure chest. Participants select magazine pictures depicting treasure and glue them to poster board. Children name each treasured object.

Treasure Box Painting
Provide small wooden boxes purchased at a craft store (1 per child), craft paints and brushes. Children create their own treasure chests. Provide paint smocks, drop cloth and paper towels for clean-up. Children name what they might put in their boxes. Children can also name chosen colors as well as other things that are the same color.

Treasure Hunt Path
Create a rectangular grid of colored foam squares (construction paper, carpet samples, foam squares) on the floor. Within the grid, make a single-color path that a child can navigate from beginning to end. Place a treasure chest, coins or pearls at the end. Children follow the path to collect treasure. Variations: color Hopscotch, color Simon Says.

Regathering 	Participants gather in a circle. Play music while passing the large Styrofoam "pearl" around the circle. When the music stops, the person holding the pearl says their own name. Group responds, "(Person's name) is treasured in the Kingdom of God." Continue until all have had a turn. Singing *Jesu, Jesu* participants bring Eucharist elements to the Celebrant then sit in a circle around the Eucharistic table.
Eucharist	**Sing: *Gather our Hearts*** **Celebration of the Eucharist** Gather our hearts, oh God. Gather our thoughts, oh God. Bring us together around you.
Dismissal 	Celebrant provides the blessing: Celebrant: "Go in Peace to Love and Serve the Lord." Participants: "Thanks be to God!" All sing and sign *Jesus Loves Me*.

Storytelling Script

Our story today is from our Bible (*show Bible*), our book that tells the stories of God and God's people, of Jesus (*show Jesus doll*), God's son, and of how much God loves us (*place hands over heart*).

Jesus spent a lot of his time going from village to village teaching people about God. Sometimes Jesus talked about the "Kingdom of God." The Kingdom of God is a place where everything is just as it should be. Everyone is cared for and happy. Everyone is included and loved and treated fairly.

The Kingdom of God is a beautiful place. It is also very precious.

Ask the following question.
"What does it mean when something is *precious*?"
Pause to hear children's answers.

When something is precious, it means that it is important to us. It is very valuable and special and we care for it.

Ask:
Can you name anything that is precious in your life?
Solicit answers (e.g. toys, possessions, clothes).
Suggest other 'precious' things (e.g. parents, pets, grandparents, the Church, Jesus.)

Jesus told two stories about the Kingdom of God and how it is precious. Jesus called these stories parables.

First, (*present treasure chest with gold coins*) Jesus said that the Kingdom of God was so precious that it was like a man who found a hidden treasure (*sift coins through fingers*).

The man wanted to keep the treasure so much that he buried it in a field. Then, he bought the field. The man knew that he could hold onto the treasure because he had buried it in the dirt. He did not want to lose his precious treasure.

Then, Jesus also said that the Kingdom of God was so precious that it was like a pearl (*present different sized pearl beads*), but not like this pearl (*pick up small pearl*), or this pearl (*pick up medium pearl*), or even this pearl (*pick up another, larger pearl*). The Kingdom of God was like *this* pearl. *Present giant styrofoam pearl, previously hidden.*

The Kingdom of God something so special, so valuable, so precious that we want to have it forever.

Jesus invites *us* to come into the Kingdom of God, where everything is beautiful. We are invited because God believes that we are precious, too.

God knows us and loves us and wants us to be part of this beautiful Kingdom. When we close our eyes and say a prayer to God, we are in the Kingdom of God. The Kingdom of God is not a place, but a feeling—a feeling of being loved, of knowing that we are safe and welcomed and that God is at our side.

God loves us and wants us to know that we are precious.

Amen.

After an appropriate pause, the Storyteller goes on to explain the activities of the day.

Rhythms of Grace • March Year 1

Theme: Jesus' ever present power calms and protects us.

Scripture: Jesus stills the storm. (Mark 4:35-41)

Date: _____

Location: _____

Volunteer Roles:

Facilitator _____

Storyteller _____

Celebrant _____

Center Leader _____

Guide _____

Items Needed for this Session

❏ **Gathering** ❏ (no supplies needed)

❏ **Storytelling** ❏ Bible, Jesus doll ❏ Storytelling Script, Story Cards

❏ **Exploring**

Creating Waves
❏ textured shelf paper
❏ blue gel shave cream
❏ plastic cover for table

Water Table: The Storm
❏ water table or large plastic storage bin, water
❏ toy boats
❏ vinegar and baking soda
❏ dish soap

Storm in a Bottle
❏ salt
❏ blue food coloring
❏ teaspoon
❏ marker
❏ dish washing liquid
❏ empty plastic 2 liter soda bottles with caps (1 per child)

Blindfold Maze
❏ blindfold (optional)
❏ obstacles (chairs, pillows, tall table)

❏ **Regathering** ❏ parachute or large bed sheet ❏ elements for the Eucharistic table (see Eucharist)

❏ **Eucharist**
❏ altar table and elements (pita bread, juice, chalice, paten, purificator, corporal, altar cloth)
❏ Bible and Jesus doll
❏ Eucharistic Prayer (see p. 100)
❏ *Gather our Hearts* song lyrics (see p. 99)

❏ **Dismissal** ❏ *Jesus Loves Me* song lyrics (see p. 99)

❏ **Leaders and Aides Pre-service:** Set up space. Finalize details. Pray.
❏ **Leaders and Aides Post-service:** Clean-up and share feedback. Set dates, discuss theme for next month.

Rhythms of Grace

Today's Theme:	Jesus' ever present power calms and protects us.
Today's Scripture:	Jesus stills the storm. (Mark 4:35-41)

Our Worship Service

Gathering

Explore the authority of Jesus to bring calm to our troubled lives with this adaptation of a familiar children's game.

Storytelling

Today we hear the story of Jesus teaching about faith by calming the waters.

Exploring

Creating Waves
Participants get a hands-on experience of making waves with shave cream.
(*sensory integration, gross motor*)

Water Table: The Storm
Children explore storms in this water table activity.
(*gross motor, sensory integration, communication*)

Storm in a Bottle
Participants enjoy creating a whirlwind storm in a bottle.
(*gross motor, fine motor, kinesthetic awareness*)

Blindfold Maze
Individuals practice trusting others in navigating difficult terrain.
(*gross motor, communication, kinesthetic awareness*)

Regathering

Come together in another game of Jesus Says.
Sing *Jesu, Jesu*.
We bring elements of the Eucharist to the Celebrant to create the Eucharistic table.

Eucharist

Sing: *Gather our Hearts*
Gather our hearts, oh God.
Gather our thoughts, oh God.
Bring us together around you.

Celebration of the Eucharist

Dismissal

Sing and Sign: *Jesus Loves Me*
Blessing
Celebrant: "Go in Peace to Love and Serve the Lord."
Participants: "Thanks be to God!"

This Month's Session Plan

Gathering

Begin the session with a game of Jesus Says (similar to Simon Says) with participants joining as they arrive. When Facilitator or volunteer says, "Jesus says jump on both feet," all participants jump until the Facilitator or volunteer says, "Peace, be still." Continue until Gathering time is over.

Storytelling

Theme: Jesus' ever present power calms and protects us.
See Storytelling Script on the following page. Prepare Story Cards for Storytelling (Appendix I, pp. 103-104).
Place the Bible and the Jesus doll by the Storyteller.

Exploring

Creating Waves
Dispense an egg-sized portion of blue gel shave cream for each child. Children use their hands to swirl shave cream into waves on textured shelf paper.

Water Table: The Storm
(*Option 1*) Place vinegar and a small amount of baking soda in the water table Invite children to observe the chemical-reaction storm.
(*Option 2: Some children have an aversion to the smell of vinegar.*) Fill a water table with an inch depth of plain water and a small amount of dish soap. Children create storms of waves and bubbles.
Invite children to play with toy boats, reenacting the story of Jesus calming the waters.

Storm in a Bottle
Fill empty plastic 2-liter soda bottles 2/3 full of water, 1 per child. Add teaspoon of salt, one drop of dish-washing liquid, and several drops of blue food coloring to each. Replace bottle caps. Children shake bottles with both hands, moving in a circular motion. The mixture will form a funnel. Children write their name on containers to take home.

Blindfold Maze
Using objects from the room, create a custom obstacle course/maze tailored to the needs of each participant. Blindfold each participant (or ask participants to simply close their eyes), then guide each through the maze with verbal directions and by hand holding. Afterwards, invite each child to talk about the experience.

Regathering

Participants come together holding the edge of a parachute or large sheet for a game of Jesus Says (based on Simon Says). Leader gives series of directions that children follow only if prefaced by "Jesus Says." (e.g. Jesus says, "Make waves," "Hide underneath," "Move left.") Depending on participant ability, you may choose to only give "Jesus says," directives. Continue as long as interest is maintained.
Singing *Jesu, Jesu* participants bring Eucharist elements to the Celebrant then sit in a circle around the Eucharistic table.

Eucharist

Sing: *Gather our Hearts*
Gather our hearts, oh God.
Gather our thoughts, oh God.
Bring us together around you.

Celebration of the Eucharist

Dismissal

All sing and sign *Jesus Loves Me*.
Celebrant provides the blessing:
Celebrant: "Go in Peace to Love and Serve the Lord."
Participants: "Thanks be to God!"

Storytelling Script

Place the Bible and the Jesus doll by the Storyteller.
Today's Storytelling uses the three Story Cards for this session found in Appendix 1, pp. 103-104.
1. Jesus and disciples on boat (March • Year 1 • 1 of 3)
2. The boat in the storm (March • Year 1 • 2 of 3)
3. Jesus calms the waters (March • Year 1 • 3 of 3)

Our story today is from our Bible (*show Bible*), our book that tells the stories of God and God's people, of Jesus (*show Jesus doll*), God's son, and of how much God loves us (*place hands over heart*).

Today's story is from the second part of our Bible.
Show Bible and divide it in half by placing your hand between the left and right halves.
The second part of our Bible is called the New Testament. It has the stories of Jesus.

One day when Jesus had spent a good part of the day helping people and teaching them how to have a better life, he began to get tired. He said to his special friends, his disciples, "Let's take this boat to the other side of the lake." They all got into the boat and began across the lake. *Show the first story card. Place the card in view of the children.*

The evening was quiet and relaxing for both Jesus and the disciples. Jesus fell asleep. But, suddenly, about half way across the lake, the wind began to whip against the sail. The sky grew dark and thunder, lightening, and rain rocked the boat. *Show and place the second story card next to the first.*

The disciples were terrified. They could do nothing to steady the boat. They all thought that the boat was going to sink! They yelled to Jesus, who was asleep, "Help us, we are going to drown!" Jesus got up and calmly said, "Peace, be still." *Show and place the third story card.*

As soon as Jesus spoke, the sea went still, the wind stopped blowing, the rain, thunder and lightening stopped, the sun came out and all was peaceful again. The disciples were amazed. Jesus said to his friends, "Why are you so afraid, don't you have any faith?" Jesus had taken care of them.

Amen.

After an appropriate pause, the Storyteller goes on to explain the activities of the day.

Rhythms of Grace • April Year 1

Theme: Depending on what we need, Jesus can be many things to us.

Scripture: The "I Am" statements (John 8:12; 6:35, 48-51; 15:1-7)

Date: _____

Location: _____

Volunteer Roles:

Facilitator _____

Storyteller _____

Celebrant _____

Center Leader _____

Guide _____

Items Needed for this Session

❏ **Gathering**
- ❏ large kraft paper banner hung on wall, tape
- ❏ markers, crayons, colored pencils

❏ **Storytelling**
- ❏ Bible, Jesus doll
- ❏ Storytelling Script
- ❏ small lamp, shade removed
- ❏ candle, matches or lighter (optional)
- ❏ pita bread
- ❏ artificial grape vine

❏ **Exploring**

Candle Making
- ❏ sheets of colored beeswax for candle making
- ❏ cotton wicks
- ❏ glitter or sequins

Bread-Dough Play
- ❏ pre-made bread dough (defrosted)
- ❏ flour
- ❏ cookie sheets
- ❏ non-stick spray
- ❏ an oven for baking

Dinner Roll Toss
- ❏ 6 stale dinner rolls
- ❏ cooking pots or baskets (2 or 3)

Vine and Branches
- ❏ 6' length of artificial grapevine
- ❏ purple construction paper grapes (4" dia.)
- ❏ tape or string
- ❏ crayons, markers or colored pencils

Pipe cleaner vines
- ❏ brown pipe cleaners
- ❏ segments of artificial foliage

❏ **Regathering**
- ❏ elements for the Eucharistic table (see Eucharist)
- ❏ an example from Gathering activities of a candle, a dinner roll and a grapevine
- ❏ recorded music, player

❏ **Eucharist**
- ❏ altar table and elements (pita bread, juice, chalice, paten, purificator, corporal, altar cloth)
- ❏ Bible and Jesus doll
- ❏ Eucharistic Prayer (see p. 100)
- ❏ *Gather our Hearts* song lyrics (see p. 99)

❏ **Dismissal**
- ❏ *Jesus Loves Me* song lyrics (see p. 99)

❏ **Leaders and Aides Pre-service:** Set up space. Finalize details. Pray.

❏ **Leaders and Aides Post-service:** Clean-up and share feedback. Set dates, discuss theme for next month.

Rhythms of Grace

Today's Theme:	Depending on what we need, Jesus can be many things to us.
Today's Scripture:	The "I Am" statements (John 8:12; 6:35, 48-51; 15:1-7)

Our Worship Service

Gathering

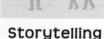

Symbolize our togetherness and community in Christ with a banner naming and depicting each person.

Storytelling

Today we hear Jesus tell us who he "is" in our lives.
"I am the light of the world." "I am the bread of life." "I am the vine, you are the branches."

Exploring

Candle Making
Participants explore Jesus as "the light of the world" by fashioning candles from rolled beeswax.
(*fine motor, communication, sensory integration*)

Bread Dough Play
Children make their own bread to connect with the notion of Jesus as the "bread of life."
(*gross motor, sensory integration*)

Dinner Roll Toss
Individuals use large motor skills to remember Jesus as the "bread of life."
(*gross motor, kinesthetic awareness*)

Vine and Branches
Participants learn that "we are the fruit and Jesus is the vine" through a name-craft activity.
(*fine motor, communication*)

Pipe cleaner Vines
Children symbolize "Jesus the vine" with lengths of pipe cleaner and silk ivy.
(*fine motor*)

Regathering

We explore symbols of the "I am" statements with a variation of Musical Chairs.
Sing *Jesu, Jesu*.
We bring elements of the Eucharist to the Celebrant to create the Eucharistic table.

Eucharist

Sing: *Gather our Hearts*
Gather our hearts, oh God.
Gather our thoughts, oh God.
Bring us together around you.

Celebration of the Eucharist

Dismissal

Sing and Sign: *Jesus Loves Me*
Blessing
Celebrant: "Go in Peace to Love and Serve the Lord."
Participants: "Thanks be to God!"

This Month's Session Plan

Gathering

Before the session, create a large kraft paper banner, hang on a wall. Draw in names and likenesses of volunteers and aides. Participants add names and draw pictures of themselves on the banner as they arrive. Provide assistance as necessary. Help participants to name colors, body parts, relationships between individuals, etc.

Storytelling

Theme: Depending on what we need, Jesus can be many things to us.
See Storytelling Script on the following page.
Place the Bible, Jesus doll, small lamp and/or candle (with matches), pita and artificial grapevine by the Storyteller.

Exploring

Candle Making
Lay sheets of colored beeswax on table. Place a segment of cotton wick at one end of the wax and gently roll candle, enclosing wick, tapering at one end. Very gently press sequins or glitter onto the outer surface of the candle. Encourage color identification as candles are made.

Bread Dough Play
Participants knead, press, roll, stretch and shape baseball-sized pieces of ready-made bread dough into small rolls. Use small amount of flour to keep dough from sticking to work surface. Keep children from eating raw dough. Place on cookie sheets sprayed with non-stick spray. Bake and send home with children.

Dinner Roll Toss
Set up several baskets of various sizes 8 to 10 feet from start. Use stale rolls as objects for tossing. Invite participants to toss rolls into baskets. Retrieve rolls and pass back for continued play.

Vine and Branches
Within children's reach hang a length of artificial grapevine. Provide children with palm-sized purple construction paper "grapes" on which they write their own names. Hang grapes on the vine with tape or string.

Pipe cleaner Vines
Invite children to create vines by twisting pipe cleaners together with lengths of silk ivy.

Regathering

Participants gather in a circle. Distribute symbols of the three "I am" statements (candle, roll, grapevine—from the Gathering activities above). Play a selection of lively music while objects are passed around the circle. When the music stops (as in Musical Chairs) the three individuals holding the symbol objects each call out the respective sentence: Candle: "Jesus is the Light of the World!" Roll: "Jesus is the Bread of Life!" Grapevine: "Jesus is the Vine" After each round, music resumes and play continues.
Singing *Jesu, Jesu* participants bring Eucharist elements to the Celebrant then sit in a circle around the Eucharistic table.

Eucharist

Sing: *Gather our Hearts*
Gather our hearts, oh God.
Gather our thoughts, oh God.
Bring us together around you.

Celebration of the Eucharist

Dismissal

All sing and sign *Jesus Loves Me*.
Celebrant provides the blessing:
Celebrant: "Go in Peace to Love and Serve the Lord."
Participants: "Thanks be to God!"

storytelling Script

Our story today is from our Bible (*show Bible*), our book that tells the stories of God and God's people, of Jesus (*show Jesus doll*), God's son, and of how much God loves us (*place hands over heart*).

In the Bible, Jesus tries to get people to understand how much he loves them and wants to help them.

The people do not know who this "Jesus" man is. He is the son of Mary. He is a carpenter from Nazareth, but he also has been moving around the country teaching people about God, healing people and performing miracles.

Lots of people have started to follow Jesus because he makes them feel better. He makes their sicknesses go away. He talks about a new kind of world where everyone is loved and equal. Everyone wants to be near him.

When Jesus' friends wanted to know more about him, he told them this:
Hold up the lamp.
"I am the light of the world."
Switch the lamp on.
Jesus said that no matter how dark it got, he would always be there for us to show us the way. He would be like a lamp in the dark night.
This is the reason we have candles in church—to remind us that Jesus is the Light of the World.

(*Optional:*
But, when Jesus lived there weren't lamps, so Jesus' friends thought of him like the flame of a candle.
If it is safe with the assembled group, light the candle briefly to display its glow.
Say it with me: "Jesus is the Light of the World."
Extinguish the candle. Place the candle down in front of the Storyteller.)

Jesus also said:
Hold up a piece of pita bread.
"I am the bread of life."
Place bread to nose and inhale.

Jesus told his friends that he could fill them up, with good ideas and with love—like bread fills us up at the kitchen table. In a little while, we will be sharing bread at Communion and sharing Jesus, the bread of life.

Say it with me:
"Jesus is the bread of life."
Place pita bread down near the lamp (and/or candle).

And Jesus told his friends:
Hold up the grapevine.
"I am the vine and you are the branches and the fruit."
Point out the different parts: vine, branches, fruit.

Jesus is the beginning of everything that we do. He is the strong vine and we grow from him and his teachings. We are the fruit, because we are the good things that come from Jesus' teachings.

Say it with me:
"Jesus is the vine. We are the branches and the fruit."
Place the vine down near the other objects.

Jesus is so many things to us. But in all of it, Jesus is love.

Amen.

After an appropriate pause, the Storyteller goes on to explain the activities of the day.

Rhythms of Grace • May Year 1

Theme:	Jesus is alive! We have seen him!
Scripture:	Mary and the Gardener (John 20:13-18)
	Road to Emmaus (Luke 24:13-33)
	Fishing for Breakfast (John 21:1-14)
Date:	_____
Location:	_____

Volunteer Roles:

Facilitator _____

Storyteller _____

Celebrant _____

Center Leader _____

Guide _____

Items Needed for this Session

❏ **Gathering**
- ❏ plants, small plastic gardening tools, dirt
- ❏ sandals, loaf of bread
- ❏ rocks, logs, fish-shapes, a fishing net

❏ **Storytelling**
- ❏ Bible, Jesus doll
- ❏ Storytelling Script, Story Cards, and Story Script Cards
- ❏ props for each story from Gathering
- ❏ (optional) additional props for each story vignette (eg. taped roadway, rocks and logs, beach sand)

❏ **Exploring**

Water Table: Let's Go Fishing
- ❏ water table or large plastic storage bin, water
- ❏ fish-shapes made from kitchen sponges (assorted colors)
- ❏ kitchen strainer or aquarium net

Fish Gathering
- ❏ fish net, large
- ❏ fish shapes made from plastic or papier maché
- ❏ large basket

Road Maze
- ❏ crawling tunnel
- ❏ furniture cushions, blankets
- ❏ large appliance boxes

Flower Garden
- ❏ pipe cleaners
- ❏ rectangles of colored tissue paper
- ❏ pinking shears
- ❏ dirt table or large plastic bin, potting soil (or styrofoam block)

❏ **Regathering**
- ❏ three easily identifiable objects (apple, ball, rock)
- ❏ three paper bags
- ❏ elements for the Eucharistic table (see Eucharist)

❏ **Eucharist**
- ❏ altar table and elements (pita bread, juice, chalice, paten, purificator, corporal, altar cloth)
- ❏ Bible and Jesus doll
- ❏ Eucharistic Prayer (see p.100)
- ❏ Gather our Hearts song lyrics (see p.99)

❏ **Dismissal**
- ❏ Jesus Loves Me song lyrics (see p.99)

❏ **Leaders and Aides Pre-service:** Set up space. Finalize details. Pray.
❏ **Leaders and Aides Post-service:** Clean-up and share feedback. Set dates, discuss theme for next month.

Rhythms of Grace

Today's Theme:	Jesus is alive! We have seen him!
Today's Scripture:	Mary and the Gardener (John 20:13-18), Road to Emmaus (Luke 24:13-33), Fishing for Breakfast (John 21:1-14)

Our Worship Service

Gathering

Begin to sort out the meaning of the resurrection appearance stories by sorting out the elements we'll use to tell these stories.

Storytelling

Today we hear stories about Jesus' resurrection appearances.

Exploring

Water Table: Let's Go Fishing
Children explore boats, fish and fishermen using water play.
(*fine motor, sensory integration*)

Fish Gathering
Pairs of children work together to gather fish into nets.
(*gross motor, communication, kinesthetic awareness*)

Road Maze
Children find the way and find each other on the way through a road maze.
(*gross motor, kinesthetic awareness, communication*)

Flower Garden
Participants take the role of gardener by creating their own flower craft.
(*fine motor, sensory integration*)

Regathering

As we come back together, we practice using word clues to identify hidden objects.
Sing *Jesu, Jesu*.
We bring elements of the Eucharist to the Celebrant to create the Eucharistic table.

Eucharist

Sing: *Gather our Hearts*
Gather our hearts, oh God.
Gather our thoughts, oh God.
Bring us together around you.

Celebration of the Eucharist

Dismissal

Sing and Sign: *Jesus Loves Me*
Blessing
Celebrant: "Go in Peace to Love and Serve the Lord."
Participants: "Thanks be to God!"

This Month's Session Plan

Gathering
Have the items (at least 1 item per person) used in today's Storytelling gathered together in one central location. As participants arrive, invite each to take one item to the location where it will be used in today's story. Ask each person to wonder what the items represent, or how items are related. When all items are distributed to the three locations, begin the story.

Storytelling
Theme: Jesus is alive! We have seen him!
See Storytelling Script on the following page. Prepare Story Cards and Script Cards (Appendix I, pp. 105-107) for Storytelling.
Place the Bible and the Jesus doll with the Storyteller. Remaining props should be in their correct locations following the Gathering activity.
The Storyteller tells the introductory death and resurrection story. Different volunteers tell the remaining 3 story vignettes. Participants move together from story to story.

Exploring

Water Table: Let's Go Fishing
Fill a water table/plastic storage bin with warm water. Place fish cut from colored sponges in the water. Children name colors and then catch the fish with net/strainer.

Fish Gathering
Lay out large fish net on the floor. Children work in pairs to load net with fish, then gather the net and drop the fish into the basket.

Road Maze
Set up a maze using large appliance boxes, cushions, cloth-draped furniture or crawling tunnels. Children crawl through the maze.

Flower Garden
Cut tissue paper of various colors into 5" x 7" rectangles with pinking shears. Make stacks of 4-6 pieces. Accordion pleat the tissue paper. Wind a pipe cleaner around the middle, across the pleats. Leave enough for a stem. Separate each layer by gently pulling upwards toward the middle of the flower. "Plant" completed flowers in potting soil or Styrofoam block.

Regathering
Place objects in paper bags. Give verbal clues for identifying each item. Participants make guesses. Continue adding clues until items are recognized.
Singing *Jesu, Jesu* participants bring Eucharist elements to the Celebrant then sit in a circle around the Eucharistic table.

Eucharist

Sing: *Gather our Hearts*
Gather our hearts, oh God.
Gather our thoughts, oh God.
Bring us together around you.

Celebration of the Eucharist

Dismissal
All sing and sign *Jesus Loves Me*.
Celebrant provides the blessing:
Celebrant: "Go in Peace to Love and Serve the Lord."
Participants: "Thanks be to God!"

Storytelling Script

Our story today is from our Bible (*show Bible*), our book that tells the stories of God and God's people, of Jesus (*show Jesus doll*), God's son, and of how much God loves us (*place hands over heart*).

Briefly tell the story of Jesus' death and resurrection:
Even though many people followed Jesus and his teachings, there were many powerful people who did not like what Jesus had to say.

Jesus was arrested and killed. But Jesus was God's son and God did something marvelous.

Three days after Jesus died, he rose from the dead because God's love was so powerful Jesus was given a new kind of life after he had died. It was a miracle!

We know Jesus rose from the dead because we have the stories from our Bible (*pick up the Bible*) in the New Testament, the story of Jesus and his friends.

Now, we are going to hear some of the stories of how Jesus' friends saw, talked with, and shared a meal with him after he rose from the dead.

Come with me....
Walk to where a volunteer is sitting ready with the assembled props to tell the story of Mary and the Gardener.

A volunteer tells the story.
End with the refrain: Jesus was alive and she had seen him!

Pause briefly after the telling of the story. Then, move with the group to the location for the Road to Emmaus story.

A second volunteer tells this story.
End with the refrain: Jesus was alive and they had seen him!

Pause briefly after the telling of the story. Then, move with the group to the location for the story of Fishing for Breakfast.

A third volunteer tells the final story.
End with the refrain: Jesus was alive and they had seen him!

Pause briefly after the telling of the story, then end the storytelling with

Amen.

After an appropriate pause, the Storyteller goes on to explain the activities of the day.

Rhythms of Grace • June Year 1

Theme: We are recipients of God's abundant gifts and caretakers of God's creation.

Scripture: Come, let us praise the Lord! (Psalm 95:1-7)

Date: _____

Location: _____

Volunteer Roles:

Facilitator _____

Storyteller _____

Celebrant _____

Center Leader _____

Guide _____

Items Needed for this Session

❏ Gathering
- ❏ Bible, Jesus doll
- ❏ Large (2' dia.) round cloth/felt "world" (Instructions in Appendix I, p. 110)
- ❏ elements of creation (jars of air, water, dirt, a plant, and sun, moon, animals and fish figures)

❏ Storytelling
- ❏ Bible, Jesus doll
- ❏ Storytelling Script
- ❏ Psalm Card (see p. 109)
- ❏ large round cloth/felt world
- ❏ elements of nature (see Gathering)
- ❏ felt cut-out figure of sun, moon, man and woman

❏ Exploring

Rock painting
- ❏ river rocks, medium-sized
- ❏ craft paint, brushes, water
- ❏ table covering, floor covering, smocks

Gratitude Cards
- ❏ 8 ½" x 11" sheets of construction paper
- ❏ pencils
- ❏ magazine pictures of things for which we are thankful
- ❏ glue
- ❏ scissors

Sand Box
- ❏ sand table or large plastic storage bin, sand
- ❏ small rocks with one- or two-word messages

Recycle Toss
- ❏ empty beverage cans
- ❏ plastic food containers
- ❏ crumpled paper
- ❏ large bucket

Globe Toss
- ❏ earth ball (inflatable globe)

❏ Regathering
- ❏ earth ball (inflatable globe)
- ❏ elements for the Eucharistic table (see Eucharist)

❏ Eucharist
- ❏ altar table and elements (pita bread, juice, chalice, paten, purificator, corporal, altar cloth)
- ❏ Bible and Jesus doll
- ❏ Eucharistic Prayer (see p. 100)
- ❏ *Gather our Hearts* song lyrics (see p. 99)

❏ Dismissal
- ❏ *Jesus Loves Me* song lyrics (see p. 99)

❏ **Leaders and Aides Pre-service:** Set up space. Finalize details. Pray.
❏ **Leaders and Aides Post-service:** Clean-up and share feedback. Set dates, discuss theme for next month.

Rhythms of Grace

Today's Theme:	We are recipients of God's abundant gifts and caretakers of God's creation.
Today's Scripture:	Come let us praise the Lord ! (Psalm 95:1-7)

Our Worship Service

Gathering

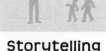

We bring together elements used in the today's creation story to symbolize the abundance of God's gifts to us.

Storytelling

Today we hear the story of God's abundant creation, and our role in caring for it.

Exploring

Rock Painting
Depict something from nature on something from nature.
(*fine motor, communication*)

Gratitude Cards
Children express their "Thanks" to God with a card.
(*fine motor, communication*)

Sand Box
Participants search for inspirational messages to share and take home.
(*communication, sensory integration, gross motor*)

Recycle Toss
Children learn about caring for God's creation through recycling.
(*gross motor, communication, kinesthetic awareness*)

Globe Toss
Explore God's creation—Earth—with a tossing and sharing game.
(*gross motor, sensory integration*)

Regathering

Recall God's ever-present love and care for us and all of creation with the song *He's Got The Whole World, In His Hands*.
We bring elements of the Eucharist to the Celebrant to create the Eucharistic table.

Eucharist

Sing: *Gather our Hearts*
Gather our hearts, oh God.
Gather our thoughts, oh God.
Bring us together around you.

Celebration of the Eucharist

Dismissal

Sing and Sign: *Jesus Loves Me*
Blessing
Celebrant: "Go in Peace to Love and Serve the Lord."
Participants: "Thanks be to God!"

This Month's Session Plan

Gathering

Before the session, use the template found in Appendix I, page 110, to create the felt world used in today's session. Distribute samples of creation elements around the worship space and place felt world in the center of the Storytelling area. Place the Jesus doll in the center of the world. Participants find samples of elements, name them and bring them to the story circle. Begin the story when participants are seated together around the felt world.

Storytelling

Theme: We are recipients of God's abundant gifts and caretakers of God's creation. Place the Bible, Jesus doll and felt world by the Storyteller. Distribute remaining props to participants.
See Storytelling Script on the following page. Prepare the Psalm Card (Appendix I, p. 109) and display it prominently in your worship space.

Exploring

Rock Painting
Supply river rocks, craft paint and brushes. Provide paint smocks, drop cloth and paper towels for clean-up. Children paint something to do with creation, (animals, ocean, trees, world) on the rocks and share their work with others.

Gratitude Cards
Fold a full piece (8 ½" x 11") of construction paper in half. Help children (if necessary) to write, "I am thankful for..." on outside of card. Discuss what children are thankful for. Help participants find a creative way (drawing, collage, words) to depict what they are thankful for on the inside of the card.

Sand Box
Before the session buy, or make small rocks with single-word inspirational messages on them (peace, love, truth, trust). Hide rocks in sand table or large plastic storage bin filled with sand. Have participants search for, find and collect the rocks. Together, read messages and select one to take home.

Recycle Toss
Introduce activity by talking about recycling and our stewardship of God's creation. Provide a selection of (clean) recyclables (paper, empty cans, plastic items) Make a game of tossing them into buckets. Then, remove and sort items into like categories.

Globe Toss
Before the session, obtain an inflatable globe or "earth ball" (available online). Participants toss earth ball around, identifying different countries, and find their home location on the map.

Regathering

Participants sing *He's Got the Whole World in His Hands* while passing earth ball (see Globe Toss) around the circle.
Continue singing as participants bring Eucharist elements to the Celebrant then sit in a circle around the Eucharistic table.

Eucharist

Sing: *Gather our Hearts*   **Celebration of the Eucharist**
Gather our hearts, oh God.
Gather our thoughts, oh God.
Bring us together around you.

Dismissal

All sing and sign *Jesus Loves Me*.
Celebrant provides the blessing:
Celebrant: "Go in Peace to Love and Serve the Lord."
Participants: "Thanks be to God!".

Storytelling Script

Begin by recalling the story of Creation:
Many, many, years ago, before any of us were born, before Jesus (*motion to Jesus doll*) was born, back to a time when there were no cars, no schools, no streets, and no T.V. ...

At the very beginning there was only God. God wanted to share God's love. So God decided to make the world!

At the very beginning, God said, "I want to share my love," and God separated the light from the darkness. God separated the water in the ocean from the water in the sky. God separated the water from the dry land. God created all the plants and the growing things. God created the lights in the sky, with the sun and the moon. God created all the creatures that swim and fly, and all the creatures on the earth.

Then, God made a man and a woman in his image.

Draw attention to the Psalm Card for today's session, and read it aloud.

Continue with the Creation story.
God told the man and the woman that they were to take care of all that came before them—
A participant places the man and woman in the middle of the felt world.

the air,
Participant places the air jar near the felt world.

the oceans and water,
Participant places the oceans and water jar near the felt world.

the dry land,
Participant places the dry land jar near the felt world.

the plants and growing things,
Participant places a plant near the felt world.

the sun and moon,
Participant places the sun and moon above the felt world.

the creatures that swim, fly and walk on the earth.
Participant places figures of animals/fish/birds near the felt world.

Once again, draw attention to the Psalm Card for today's session, and read it aloud.

God has given us all these things!
Motion to all the things around the world, and to all the participants.

We are thankful for all that God has given us.

We must take care of all of it. God has told us to take care of this world and all our gifts—including each other.

Ask:
What can you take care of ?
What else can we do to take care of what God has given us?

Amen.

After an appropriate pause, the Storyteller goes on to explain the activities of the day.

Rhythms of Grace • July Year 1

Theme: Prayer I: How we talk to God. Praying with words.

Scripture: The Lord's Prayer (Matthew 6:9-13)

Date: _____

Location: _____

Volunteer Roles:

Facilitator _____

Storyteller _____

Celebrant _____

Center Leader _____

Guide _____

Items Needed for this Session

❏ **Gathering**
- ❏ quiet music, player
- ❏ children's books with prayer theme

❏ **Storytelling**
- ❏ Bible, Jesus doll
- ❏ Storytelling Script
- ❏ dry, uncooked white rice grains,
- ❏ food coloring
- ❏ 7 bowls
- ❏ Lord's Prayer color key (Appendix I, p. 111)

❏ **Exploring**

Gratitude Prayer Garland
- ❏ yarn
- ❏ pictures of things for which we are grateful
- ❏ 4" dia. colored hearts made from construction paper
- ❏ tape
- ❏ scissors

Prayer Ball
- ❏ inflatable ball with short prayers written on it

Praying Hands
- ❏ construction paper
- ❏ crayons, markers or colored pencils

Basket of Prayers
- ❏ paper strips of one-line fill-in the blank prayers
- ❏ crayons, markers or colored pencils
- ❏ basket

❏ **Regathering**
- ❏ Lord's Prayer with hand motion hand outs (1 per participant) see p. 113
- ❏ Lord's Prayer motion poster
- ❏ elements for the Eucharistic table (see Eucharist)

❏ **Eucharist**
- ❏ altar table and elements (pita bread, juice, chalice, paten, purificator, corporal, altar cloth)
- ❏ Bible and Jesus doll
- ❏ Eucharistic Prayer (see p. 100)
- ❏ *Gather our Hearts* song lyrics (see p. 99)

❏ **Dismissal**
- ❏ *Jesus Loves Me* song lyrics (see p. 99)

❏ **Leaders and Aides Pre-service:** Set up space. Finalize details. Pray.
❏ **Leaders and Aides Post-service:** Clean-up and share feedback. Set dates, discuss theme for next month.

Rhythms of Grace

Today's Theme:	Prayer I: How we talk to God. Praying with words.
Today's Scripture:	The Lord's Prayer (Matthew 6:9-13)

Our Worship Service

Gathering

Begin today with calm, peaceful reflection and sharing with favorite Bible stories or prayers.

Storytelling

Have a real, hands-on experience with the Lord's Prayer in today's Storytelling time.

Exploring

Gratitude Prayer Garland
Children express thanks to God with a heart-string prayer garland.
(*fine motor, communication*)

Prayer Ball
Explore praying in a different way in this ball-toss game.
(*sensory integration, gross motor, kinesthetic awareness*)

Praying Hands
Have a real, hands-on experience with the Lord's Prayer in this inter-sensory prayer. (*fine motor, communication, sensory integration*)

Basket of Prayers
Pick a prayer starter, create your own prayer!
(*fine motor, communication, sensory integration*)

Regathering

Learn the words to the Lord's Prayer and a series of motions for praying it with our whole bodies.
Sing *Jesu, Jesu.*
We bring elements of the Eucharist to the Celebrant to create the Eucharistic table.

Eucharist

Sing: *Gather our Hearts*
Gather our hearts, oh God.
Gather our thoughts, oh God.
Bring us together around you.

Celebration of the Eucharist

Dismissal

Sing and Sign: *Jesus Loves Me*
Blessing
Celebrant: "Go in Peace to Love and Serve the Lord."
Participants: "Thanks be to God!"

This Month's Session Plan

Gathering

Provide quiet background music. Pair each child participant with an adult. Pairs select and read a book with Bible stories or prayers.

Storytelling

Theme: Prayer I: How we talk to God. Praying with words.
See Storytelling Script on the following page.
Place the Bible and the Jesus doll by the Storyteller.
Before the session, create bowls of colored rice with food coloring according to the Lord's Prayer color key (Appendix I, p. 111).

Exploring

Gratitude Prayer Garland

Before the session, collect pictures of things for which we are thankful. Make colored hearts from construction paper (1 per participant), attach a length of yarn to each heart. Children pick pictures of things they are thankful for and attach with tape to the yarn. Identify items, and together say a short prayer of thanks for each.

Prayer Ball

Before the session, write short prayers on an inflatable ball. Children take turns tossing the ball and reading a prayer. Continue until all have had a chance.

Praying Hands

Provide colored construction paper and crayons, markers or colored pencils. Children trace their hand on construction paper. For each finger on the tracing, ask the participant to name someone to pray for (if participants are not able, give suggestions) and either volunteer or participant labels the finger on the construction paper with each name given.

Basket of Prayers

Create one-line prayers with a fill-in-the-blank ending, for example, "God, I am happy about _____," or "God I am worried about_____." Write prayers on paper strips. Place strips in a basket. Participants draw strips from a basket, randomly, then read and complete the prayer.

Regathering

Before the session, make copies (1 per participant) of the Lord's Prayer hand-out (Appendix I, p. 113) and enlarge the handout to create one poster-sized visual aide for group use. Explain, "Sometimes having actions with words we are trying to remember can help us." Participants practice each motion with the corresponding words. Begin slowly, mastering the motions for each phrase first before moving on to the next. Work toward being able to say the entire prayer with the corresponding hand motions. Provide handout so that children may continue to practice the prayer at home.
Singing *Jesu, Jesu* participants bring Eucharist elements to the Celebrant, then sit in a circle around the Eucharistic table.

Eucharist

Sing: *Gather our Hearts*
Gather our hearts, oh God.
Gather our thoughts, oh God.
Bring us together around you.

Celebration of the Eucharist

Dismissal

All sing and sign *Jesus Loves Me*.
Celebrant provides the blessing:
Celebrant: "Go in Peace to Love and Serve the Lord."
Participants: "Thanks be to God!"

Storytelling Script

Our story today is from our Bible (*show Bible*), our book that tells the stories of God and God's people, of Jesus (*show Jesus doll*), God's son, and of how much God loves us (*place hands over heart*).

Prayer is a way that we spend time with our friend, God. Prayer is a way to talk with God, to share our thoughts with God and to listen quietly for God. God is always there to talk with us.

Jesus invites us to draw near to God. "Teach us how to pray," the disciples said to Jesus. He answered by teaching them the prayer we call the *The Lord's Prayer*. Lets listen to the parts of the Lord's Prayer and what each part means.

Volunteer: "Our Father who art in heaven," (*Pass the bowl of white rice.*)
This means we're praying to our Father who is in heaven. The prayer starts this way so we know that we're praying to God our Father and that we're not alone. God wants us to talk to him like we talk to our own father. God is our loving Father and we are his special children.

Volunteer: "Hallowed be thy name." (*Pass the bowl of yellow rice.*)
This means *holy is your name*. Even though God wants us to call him our *father*, he is still God. God just wants us to remember that God is special because he is God. When we pray to him we need to be very respectful.

Volunteer: "Thy kingdom come. Thy will be done—on earth, as it is in heaven." (*Pass the bowl of blue rice.*)
If we think about where God lives, we know it's pretty great. The Bible says that in heaven there will be no more crying, God will live with us, and there will be no hunger or hurt there.

Volunteer: "Give us this day our daily bread," (*Pass the bowl of brown rice.*)
God gives us all that we need, every day. *Our daily bread* means all of the things that we can't live without—food, water and shelter—not video games or princess dolls or other things that we simply want but don't really need.

Volunteer: "And forgive us our trespasses, as we forgive the trespasses of others." (*Pass the bowl of red rice.*)
Forgiveness means that we are sorry for something we've done and we don't want to do it anymore. God also wants us to forgive people who have done wrong to us. Sometimes others hurt us very badly and this is very hard. We need to ask for God's help especially when we don't want to forgive someone.

Volunteer: "And lead us not into temptation, but deliver us from evil." (*Pass the bowl of black rice.*)
It is sometimes tempting to do something you're not supposed to. This part of the prayer is very important because it asks God to help us to know the right thing to do and protect us from the evil that is in the world.

Volunteer: "For thine is the kingdom, and the power, and the glory, forever and ever. Amen." (*Pass the bowl of purple rice.*)
The last part of the prayer is the best part! *For thine is the kingdom* means that Heaven will last forever and will always be God's. God also has all the power and all the glory FOREVER!

We can pray this prayer any time we want to talk to God and remember all the good things about our friendship with God.
(*Repeat the Lord's Prayer, all together*) Amen.

After an appropriate pause, the Storyteller goes on to explain the activities of the day.

Rhythms of Grace • August Year 1

Theme: Prayer II: How we talk to God.
Praying with actions.

Scripture: Pray Without Ceasing
(I Thessalonians 5:17-18)

Date: _____

Location: _____

Volunteer Roles:

Facilitator _____

Storyteller _____

Celebrant _____

Center Leader _____

Guide _____

Items Needed for this Session

❏ **Gathering**
- ❏ pictures of things we might pray for
- ❏ basket

❏ **Storytelling**
- ❏ Bible, Jesus doll
- ❏ Storytelling Script
- ❏ items from Gathering

❏ **Exploring**

Prayer Path
- ❏ 15-20 cardboard circles (8"-12" dia.)
- ❏ masking tape
- ❏ (*Optional*) large canvas drop cloth with labyrinth pattern on one side

Prayer Beads
- ❏ assortment of craft beads (sm., med., lg.)
- ❏ wire, string, yarn, floss
- ❏ crosses (1 per participant)
- ❏ scissors

Prayer Ribbons
- ❏ large rubber band or hair tie
- ❏ assortment of colored ribbons, various lengths
- ❏ scissors

Prayer Stations
- ❏ small table and chairs
- ❏ simple snack (crackers, juice)
- ❏ hand made (11" x 17") paper place mats
- ❏ cups, napkins, paper towels
- ❏ baby doll and doll crib
- ❏ blankets, pillows

❏ **Regathering**
- ❏ large game ball
- ❏ elements for the Eucharistic table (see Eucharist)

❏ **Eucharist**
- ❏ altar table and elements (pita bread, juice, chalice, paten, purificator, corporal, altar cloth)
- ❏ Bible and Jesus doll
- ❏ Eucharistic Prayer (see p. 100)
- ❏ *Gather our Hearts* song lyrics (see p. 99)

❏ **Dismissal**
- ❏ *Jesus Loves Me* song lyrics (see p. 99)

❏ **Leaders and Aides Pre-service:** Set up space. Finalize details. Pray.
❏ **Leaders and Aides Post-service:** Clean-up and share feedback. Set dates, discuss theme for next month.

Rhythms of Grace

Today's Theme: Prayer II: How we talk to God. Praying with actions.
Today's Scripture: Pray Without Ceasing (I Thessalonians 5:17-18)

Our Worship Service

Gathering

Begin today's story by bringing to mind things that we pray about.

Storytelling

Today's story is about praying without ceasing, or spending our lives with God.

Exploring

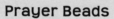

Prayer Path
Children follow a path of prayer.
(*kinesthetic awareness, communication, gross motor*)

Prayer Beads
Children create and use a simple strand of prayer beads.
(*fine motor, communication*)

Prayer Ribbons
Create colorful prayer ribbons to use in Eucharist liturgy.
(*fine motor, communication, kinesthetic awareness*)

Prayer Stations
Practice prayer with mealtime and bedtime free play.
(*communication, kinesthetic awareness, sensory integration*)

Regathering

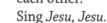

Gather together in community in anticipation of the Eucharist by offering prayers for each other.
Sing *Jesu, Jesu.*
We bring elements of the Eucharist to the Celebrant to create the Eucharistic table.

Eucharist

Sing: *Gather our Hearts*
Gather our hearts, oh God.
Gather our thoughts, oh God.
Bring us together around you.

Celebration of the Eucharist

Dismissal

Sing and Sign: *Jesus Loves Me*
Blessing
Celebrant: "Go in Peace to Love and Serve the Lord."
Participants: "Thanks be to God!"

This Month's Session Plan

Gathering

As participants arrive, they are invited to carry pictures of things we might pray for displayed on the table and put them in the large basket located in the storytelling area. Engage children in conversation, asking if they know what the item is, what it is used for, if they have something like it at home, etc.

Storytelling

Theme: Prayer II: How we talk to God. Praying with actions.
See Storytelling Script on the following page.
Place the Bible and the Jesus doll by the Storyteller.

Exploring

Prayer Path
Use "stepping stones" made of cardboard (8"-12" dia.), or create a random path out of tape on the floor of the worship space or a simple labyrinth on a large canvas drop cloth. Place several round cardboard prayer-suggestion (sick friend or loved one, something you're grateful for, etc.) circles (8"-12" dia.) along the path. Adult guide leads children along the path, encouraging prayer at each circle. Or, volunteer guides simply pray for the child at each circle.

Prayer Beads
Thread a cross onto string as if making a necklace. Next, add a spacer bead by threading both ends of the string through the bead. Add one large bead for each family member with a spacer bead between each. Knot the ends of the string. Pray the Lord's Prayer holding the cross, then offer prayers of thanks or intercession for each family member.

Prayer Ribbons
Tie various colors and lengths of ribbon pieces onto large circular rubber band or hair tie. With each color, ask child to name something in God's creation that is the same color.

Prayer Stations
Prayer at table: Create a mealtime free-play area (table, chairs, plates, implements). Set table with prayer place mats (11" x 17" sheets of paper printed with a familiar meal blessing), napkins, paper plates, crackers, juice or water. Together children say grace and share a simple snack. Discuss family mealtime prayers.
Prayer at bedtime: Create a doll crib free-play area (dolls, crib, blankets, bottles). Children pretend to put dolls to bed. When the dolls are in bed, pray, "Lord, keep us safe this night/and in everything we do. May angels guard us while we sleep 'till morning light is new."

Regathering

Provide a large ball. Participants form a circle. First child rolls the ball across the circle saying, "Dear God we pray for (name of person receiving ball)." Recipient continues by rolling ball across to another person with the same prayer. Play continues until each participant has been named and prayed for. To simplify, leader may roll ball across the circle saying "Today we pray for (person's name)." The recipient calls out their own name. Singing *Jesu, Jesu* participants bring Eucharist elements to the Celebrant then sit in a circle around the Eucharistic table.

Eucharist

Sing: *Gather our Hearts*
Gather our hearts, oh God.
Gather our thoughts, oh God.
Bring us together around you.

Celebration of the Eucharist

Dismissal

All sing and sign *Jesus Loves Me.*
Celebrant provides the blessing:
Celebrant: "Go in Peace to Love and Serve the Lord."
Participants: "Thanks be to God!".

storytelling Script

Place the Bible and Jesus doll by the Storyteller.

Our story today is from our Bible (*show Bible*), our book that tells the stories of God and God's people, of Jesus (*show Jesus doll*), God's son, and of how much God loves us (*place hands over heart*).

A long time ago, after Jesus had lived, and died, and was risen, Jesus went to live in heaven with God.

A man named Paul believed that Jesus was the Son of God and that what Jesus had started here on earth must continue. Paul knew that if we believed in Jesus as the Son of God that we, too, would someday live forever in heaven with God.

And Paul knew that what Jesus came to teach us was very important: that we must love God and that we must love our neighbors as ourselves.

Paul traveled from city to city teaching the people about Jesus and about how to live together as the people of God.

Paul taught the people, and tells us, about prayer. Paul tells us to pray without ceasing. Paul tells us to pray all day!

When we pray, we talk to God about what is important to us. There are all kinds of prayers and ways to pray.

Ask:
What are some things we might want to talk to God about?
Allow participants to respond.

We might want to thank God for something, or someone, or ourselves. We might ask God to help us do something or to be a certain way—maybe to help us take care of our pets, or to be a good friend.

Or, we may want to say we are sorry when we do things wrong or hurt someone with things we do or don't do. We can also tell God about those we are worried about—someone who is sad, or sick, or lonely. God will listen to all our prayers. God wants to have a conversation with each and every one of us.

Prayer—our conversations with God—can happen in many ways and at any time. We can pray quietly in our hearts.
Place both hands together over your heart.

We can pray out loud. *Hold both hands out, palms facing up.*

We can pray alone (*eyes closed, head down*) or with a group (*hands reaching out to others*).

We can also pray by singing, by making art, by dancing and just by playing!

We can pray in lots of different ways. We can do that when we are walking, when we are sitting, when we are dancing, at mealtime and before we go to sleep. God wants to hear what we have to say. And sometimes, we might hear God answering us.

Today, let's explore different ways to pray.

Amen.

After an appropriate pause, the Storyteller goes on to explain the activities of the day.

Rhythms of Grace • September Year 1

Theme:	Our loving God created everything.
Scripture:	The story of Creation (Genesis 1:1–2:4)
Date:	_____
Location:	_____

Volunteer Roles:

Facilitator _____

Storyteller _____

Celebrant _____

Center Leader _____

Guide _____

Items Needed for this Session

❑ Gathering
- ❑ selection of stuffed animals from Storytelling (see below.)

❑ Storytelling
- ❑ 7 paper bags, numbered 1-7, containing (#1 light bulb, #2 clear plastic bowl, #3 small bag of dirt, jar of water, silk houseplant, #4 paper cut-outs of sun, moon and stars, #5 stuffed animals: birds and fish, #6 stuffed animals: mammals, reptiles, human man, human woman, #7 blanket or pillow)
- ❑ Bible, Jesus doll
- ❑ Storytelling Script
- ❑ poster board placard with these words "It is Good, It is very Good."

❑ Exploring

Water Table: Creation Play
- ❑ water table or large plastic bin, water
- ❑ plastic sea creatures
- ❑ cups, scoops and funnels

Planting God's Garden
- ❑ large shallow plastic bin, potting soil
- ❑ small garden pots
- ❑ sticks
- ❑ flower seeds
- ❑ large spoon
- ❑ watering can
- ❑ marker

Gingerbread Creations
- ❑ pre-mixed gingerbread dough
- ❑ cookie cutters (animal and people shapes)
- ❑ rolling pin, spatula, cookie sheets
- ❑ flour
- ❑ sandwich bags
- ❑ an oven for baking

Leaf Rubbings
- ❑ assortment of fresh green leaves
- ❑ large crayons
- ❑ plain white paper

❑ Regathering
- ❑ earth ball (inflatable globe)
- ❑ elements for the Eucharistic table (see Eucharist)

❑ Eucharist
- ❑ altar table and elements (pita bread, juice, chalice, paten, purificator, corporal, altar cloth)
- ❑ Bible and Jesus doll
- ❑ Eucharistic Prayer (see p. 100)
- ❑ *Gather our Hearts* song lyrics (see p. 99)

❑ Dismissal
- ❑ *Jesus Loves Me* song lyrics (see p. 99)

❑ Leaders and Aides Pre-service: Set up space. Finalize details. Pray.

❑ Leaders and Aides Post-service: Clean-up and share feedback. Set dates, discuss theme for next month.

Rhythms of Grace

Today's Theme:	Our loving God created everything.
Today's Scripture:	The story of Creation (Genesis 1:1–2:4)

Our Worship Service

Gathering

Begin today's session by identifying and imitating some of the animals in God's creation.

Storytelling

Today's story is about all the wonderful things God has made for us.

Exploring

Water Table: Creation Play
Learn about water and sea creatures through this water-table activity.
(*sensory integration, communication*)

Planting God's Garden
Participate in the abundance of God's creation by nurturing plant seeds.
(*sensory integration, fine motor*)

Gingerbread Creations
Create human figures and animals from gingerbread cookie dough.
(*fine motor, sensory integration, kinesthetic awareness*)

Leaf Rubbings
The beauty of God's creation comes through in this leaf craft activity.
(*fine motor, communication*)

Regathering

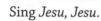

Play a naming and turn-taking game that thanks God for all of creation—ourselves included!
Sing *Jesu, Jesu.*
We bring elements of the Eucharist to the Celebrant to create the Eucharistic table.

Eucharist

Sing: *Gather our Hearts*
Gather our hearts, oh God.
Gather our thoughts, oh God.
Bring us together around you.

Celebration of the Eucharist

Dismissal

Sing and Sign: *Jesus Loves Me*
Blessing
Celebrant: "Go in Peace to Love and Serve the Lord."
Participants: "Thanks be to God!"

This Month's Session Plan

Gathering

Provide access to the stuffed animals listed for the Storytelling activity. Arriving participants play with stuffed animals. Engage children in identifying animals and mimicking animal sounds.

Storytelling

Theme: Our loving God created everything.
See Storytelling Script on the following page.
Place the Bible and the Jesus doll by the Storyteller.
Before the session, prepare the materials in separate bags, label #1-#7. Place bags by the Storyteller. Create poster board placard saying: It is good. It is very good!

Exploring

Water Table: Creation Play

In addition to the water table, provide plastic sea creatures as well as funnels, scoops and cups for filling and pouring. Children identify various sea creatures and create their own free-play scenarios.

Planting God's Garden

Provide supply of potting soil in a shallow plastic bin, and small garden pots (1 per child). Participants fill pots with soil. Lightly pack dirt and poke holes for seeds using chopstick or pencil. Add seeds. Cover gently with soil. Water pots using a watering can. Mark pots with child's name. Send pots home to care for and watch grow.

Gingerbread Creations

Provide pre-mixed gingerbread dough. Sprinkle table surface with small amount of flour. Participants pat or roll flat small portions of dough. Using cookie cutters, children form cookies in animal and gingerbread-people shapes. Bake cookies and put in sandwich bags to take home. Prevent children from eating raw dough, and keep children at a safe distance from the oven.

Leaf Rubbings

Provide assortment of fresh green leaves. Place a piece of plain white paper over leaf and rub on paper surface with crayons of various colors to create colorful leaf pictures.

Regathering

Provide an earth ball (inflatable globe). Participants sit in a circle. Leader begins by saying "God made so many things in our world. Let's pray to God and thank God for all that God has made." Leader chooses a general category (animals, foods, plants), and as participants roll the earth ball across the circle, they name something from that category (animals: giraffes) and offer a prayer of thanks (Thank you God, for giraffes!). Recipient continues by rolling, naming and thanking God for something else in the general category. Finish the game by naming *us* as the general category. Name and thank God for each person present. Simplify the game by only playing the last round, naming each other and thanking God for each person.
Singing *Jesu, Jesu* participants bring Eucharist elements to the Celebrant then sit in a circle around the Eucharistic table.

Eucharist

Sing: *Gather our Hearts*

Gather our hearts, oh God.
Gather our thoughts, oh God.
Bring us together around you.

Celebration of the Eucharist

Dismissal

All sing and sign *Jesus Loves Me*.
Celebrant provides the blessing:
Celebrant: "Go in Peace to Love and Serve the Lord."
Participants: "Thanks be to God!"

Storytelling Script

Place the Bible, Jesus doll, "It is Good" placard and bags of story props by the Storyteller.

Our story today is from our Bible (*show Bible*), our book that tells the stories of God and God's people, of Jesus (*show Jesus doll*), God's son, and of how much God loves us (*place hands over heart*).

This story begins a long time before you or I were born. This story goes back even to the time before Jesus (*indicate Jesus doll*) was born.

This story goes back to a time when there were no cars, no skateboards, no schools, no streets, no TVs. This story starts at the very beginning when God made the world!

The people who wrote the Bible say that God made the world in seven days, and that on each day, something new was made.

Let's look inside this bag with the number *1* on it and see what God made on the very first day.
Storyteller invites a participant to open the bag and to take out the contents, showing the group.

Say:
Hmmm, a light bulb, God made light on the very first day. It was all darkness at the beginning of time and God said, "Let there be light," and there was light. And then, looking at the light, God said, "It is good."

Invite children to repeat:
"It is good. It is very good!"

Storyteller puts object on rug and discards bag to the side. Repeat for bags #2-#6, ending each time with "It is good. It is very good!" After bag number 6, say:
And then, after 6 days, God was done. God had made, (*review items from bags*), light, the sky, earth and water…"

Ask:
What do you suppose God did next?
Motion to remaining paper bag, #7 and invite answers.

Let's see!
Open bag #7 containing a pillow and/or a blanket.
God rested!

And God said—looking at all of Creation: (*have children join in refrain*) "It is good. It is very good!"

Amen.

After an appropriate pause, the Storyteller goes on to explain the activities of the day.

Rhythms of Grace • October Year 1

Theme: We are all part of God's big family.

Scripture: The Story of Abraham
(Genesis 15:1-6, 17:1-9, 18:1-15)

Date: _____

Location: _____

Volunteer Roles:

Facilitator _____

Storyteller _____

Celebrant _____

Center Leader _____

Guide _____

Items Needed for this Session

❏ **Gathering**
- ❏ star shapes made of poster board (4" dia.)
- ❏ ball of yarn or string
- ❏ hole punch
- ❏ large paper clips
- ❏ (*optional*) step stool

❏ **Storytelling**
- ❏ Bible, Jesus doll
- ❏ Storytelling Script, Story Cards

❏ **Exploring**

Star Pictures
- ❏ star shapes made of poster board (4" dia.)
- ❏ digital camera and photo printer or Polaroid ® instant camera
- ❏ decorating supplies
- ❏ string
- ❏ hole punch
- ❏ marker
- ❏ letter stencils
- ❏ craft paint
- ❏ star-shaped sponges (4" dia.)

Guests for Dinner
- ❏ table, table cloth
- ❏ plastic cups, dishes, utensils
- ❏ small basket

Matching the Stars
- ❏ several styles of star pairs (clip art, books, magazines, free-hand)

Names Poster
- ❏ book of baby names
- ❏ white paper (11" x 17")
- ❏ marker

❏ **Regathering**
- ❏ elements for the Eucharistic table (see Eucharist)

❏ **Eucharist**
- ❏ altar table and elements (pita bread, juice, chalice, paten, purificator, corporal, altar cloth)
- ❏ Bible and Jesus doll
- ❏ Eucharistic Prayer (see p. 100)
- ❏ *Gather our Hearts* song lyrics (see p. 99)

❏ **Dismissal**
- ❏ *Jesus Loves Me* song lyrics (see p. 99)

❏ **Leaders and Aides Pre-service:** Set up space. Finalize details. Pray.
❏ **Leaders and Aides Post-service:** Clean-up and share feedback. Set dates, discuss theme for next month.

Rhythms of Grace

Today's Theme:	We are all part of God's big family.
Today's Scripture:	The Story of Abraham (Genesis 17:1-9, 18:1-15)

Our Worship Service

Gathering

Begin today's session by highlighting the stars in the sky—and the stars in the room!

Storytelling

Today's story is about being one of the many stars in God's great family.

Exploring

Star Pictures
Using photographs of themselves, participants learn that we are all "stars"—descendents of Abraham and Sarah.
(*fine motor, communication*)

Names Poster
Children and adults find and share the meanings of their own names.
(*communication, fine motor*)

Guests for Dinner
Children connect today's theme of welcome with day-to-day experience of setting the table.
(*kinesthetic awareness, gross motor, communication*)

Matching the Stars
Participants play matching and memory games with pairs of star images.
(*fine motor, sensory integration*)

Regathering

Help recall Abraham's large family with a light and playful game/song.
Sing *Jesu, Jesu*.
We bring elements of the Eucharist to the Celebrant to create the Eucharistic table.

Eucharist

Sing: *Gather our Hearts*
Gather our hearts, oh God.
Gather our thoughts, oh God.
Bring us together around you.

Celebration of the Eucharist

Dismissal

Sing and Sign: *Jesus Loves Me*
Blessing
Celebrant: "Go in Peace to Love and Serve the Lord."
Participants: "Thanks be to God!"

This Month's Session Plan

Gathering	Before the session, stretch string across worship space or story area just above participant's heads, and create star shapes from poster board; punch holes in stars, add strings and large paper clips for hooks. Arrange stars on the floor. Participants choose stars and hang them on the strings. Provide step stool or assistance as required.
Storytelling	Theme: We are all part of God's big family. See Storytelling Script on the following page. Prepare Story Cards for Storytelling. (Appendix I, pp. 115-116). Place the Bible and the Jesus doll with the Storyteller.

Exploring

Star Pictures

Cut out stars from poster board, at least one per participant. On one side write "A Star of Abraham." Take and print a picture of each person. Trim to size and glue to stars. Invite participants to decorate stars with glitter or other craft items. Punch hole in star and string with yarn.

Names Poster

In a book of baby names, find the name of each individual. Write each name with its definition beneath on 11" x 17" paper. Decorate with craft paint and sponge stars.

Guests for Dinner

Participants set a table with plates, cups, spoons, forks, tablecloth, flowers, etc. Talk about what the items are and what we use them for when we eat. Talk about what it means to welcome someone as a guest. Share welcoming stories and experiences. Then, clear the table and put items back in basket.

Matching the Stars

Find or create matched pairs of star images (drawings, photographs, illustrations). Create pairs of cards for the game. Participants play matching games or "concentration" memory games.

Regathering 	Participants sing *Father Abraham Had Seven Sons* including acting out all of the various movements. Finish with "all sit down." Singing *Jesu, Jesu* participants bring Eucharist elements to the Celebrant then sit in a circle around the Eucharistic table.

Eucharist

Sing: *Gather our Hearts*
Gather our hearts, oh God.
Gather our thoughts, oh God.
Bring us together around you.

Celebration of the Eucharist

Dismissal 	All sing and sign *Jesus Loves Me*. Celebrant provides the blessing: Celebrant: "Go in Peace to Love and Serve the Lord." Participants: "Thanks be to God!".

Storytelling Script

Place the Bible and Jesus doll by the Storyteller.
Today's Storytelling uses the three Story Cards for this session found in Appendix I, pp. 115-116.
1. Three visitors arrive (October • Year 1 • 1 of 3)
2. Sarah serves the fatted calf (October • Year 1 • 2 of 3)
3. Sarah and Abraham receiving the news (October • Year 1 • 3 of 3)

Our story today is from our Bible (*show Bible*), our book that tells the stories of God and God's people, of Jesus (*show Jesus doll*), God's son, and of how much God loves us (*place hands over heart*).

Today's story comes from the part of our Bible before Jesus was born. It is called the Old Testament. This is a story about a very special man who listened to God and did what God asked him to do. We could in a way call this man, Abraham, our great, great, great, great, great, great, great, great, great, grandfather!

Explain that today's story begins when Abram—his name at the beginning of this story—heard God's voice.

Abram was an old man who lived in the village of Ur and then Haran. When Abram was 75 years old, God told him to gather his family and leave his home and all his belongings. God would tell him where to go and what to do.

Abram had a very large family with nephews and nieces and workers, but Abram had no children of his own. God didn't really tell Abram where he was going, but Abram trusted God and so he left. *Ask:* How would you feel about just going without knowing where? *Allow participants to respond.*

Abram traveled and traveled for many years, always listening to where God told him to go. When Abram was 99 years old, God appeared to him. God promised that Abram would be the father of many nations. God promised to Abram than his family would grow and grow to be as "many as the stars in the sky."
Point to the stars hung in the Gathering activity.

God told him his name from then on would be *Abraham*, which means father of a *multitude*. *Explain that "multitude" means "many".*

Now as you can tell, Abraham and his wife Sarah were very, very old. Sarah was very sad because she had never had a baby of her own, but she loved Abraham and took care of him.

One day Abraham and his family had stopped traveling and had set up their tents to rest for a while. In the distance Abraham saw three men. *Show the first story card. Place the card in view of the children.*

Abraham welcomed the men calling to them to come and rest with him for a while. He called Sarah right away and said, "Help me to prepare a meal for our three guests!"
Place the second story card next to the first.

The men stayed with Abraham, ate and relaxed. Sarah watched from inside the tent wondering who these men were and if they could be messengers from God. The men told Abraham that Sarah was going to have a child.
Show and place the third story card.

Sarah heard this and laughed at the thought, "How could this happen, I am too old!" The men heard her laugh and said to her, "Is anything too wonderful for the Lord?"

All these things did come to pass. As the men predicted, Sarah had a son, named Isaac—which means "he laughs", and Abraham did have many, many, many ancestors. We are each one of them!

Amen.

After an appropriate pause, the Storyteller goes on to explain the activities of the day.

Rhythms of Grace • November Year 1

Theme: We live together in families given to us by God.

Scripture: The story of Joseph (Genesis 37:1-28)

Date: _____

Location: _____

Volunteer Roles:

Facilitator _____

Storyteller _____

Celebrant _____

Center Leader _____

Guide _____

Items Needed for this Session

❏ **Gathering**
- ❏ large coat shape made from foam board
- ❏ fabric pieces to affix to coat shape
- ❏ glue sticks

❏ **Storytelling**
- ❏ Bible, Jesus doll
- ❏ Storytelling Script, Story Cards

❏ **Exploring**

Brown Bag Coats
- ❏ brown paper grocery bags
- ❏ fabric scraps
- ❏ glue sticks

Bean-Family Matching Game
- ❏ cover for the floor
- ❏ assortment of different types of beans
- ❏ clear plastic jars for sorting

Family Collage
- ❏ pictures from magazines
- ❏ white paper (11" x 17")
- ❏ glue sticks

Parachute Toss
- ❏ parachute or large bed sheet
- ❏ beach ball or stuffed animals

❏ **Regathering**
- ❏ elements for the Eucharistic table (see Eucharist)

❏ **Eucharist**
- ❏ altar table and elements (pita bread, juice, chalice, paten, purificator, corporal, altar cloth)
- ❏ Bible and Jesus doll
- ❏ Eucharistic Prayer (see p. 100)
- ❏ *Gather our Hearts* song lyrics (see p. 99)

❏ **Dismissal**
- ❏ *Jesus Loves Me* song lyrics (see p. 99)

❏ **Leaders and Aides Pre-service:** Set up space. Finalize details. Pray.
❏ **Leaders and Aides Post-service:** Clean-up and share feedback. Set dates, discuss theme for next month.

Rhythms of Grace

Today's Theme:	We live together in families given to us by God.
Today's Scripture:	The story of Joseph (Genesis 37:1-28)

Our Worship Service

Gathering

Begin today's session by creating a replica of Joseph's special multi-colored coat.

Storytelling

Today's story is about the hurt and forgiveness that is sometimes a part of living in families.

Exploring

Brown Bag Coats
Children create coats like Joseph's.
(*fine motor, sensory integration, kinesthetic awareness*)

Family Collage
Participants create family art with collage.
(*fine motor, communication*)

Bean-Family Matching Game
Children use a sorting game to explore similarities and differences.
(*fine motor, sensory integration, communication*)

Parachute Toss
Players explore togetherness through parachute games.
(*kinesthetic awareness, communication, gross motor*)

Regathering

Sing *He's Got the Whole World In His Hands*, focusing on family members and those present.
We bring elements of the Eucharist to the Celebrant to create the Eucharistic table.
Sing *Jesu, Jesu*.

Eucharist

Sing: *Gather our Hearts*
Gather our hearts, oh God.
Gather our thoughts, oh God.
Bring us together around you.

Celebration of the Eucharist

Dismissal

Sing and Sign: *Jesus Loves Me*
Blessing
Celebrant: "Go in Peace to Love and Serve the Lord."
Participants: "Thanks be to God!"

This Month's Session Plan

Gathering	Before the session, create a large coat-shape cut-out from foam core or cardboard. On the coat, draw outlines of distinct shapes. Create corresponding shapes from colored fabric pieces or construction paper. Distribute these puzzle pieces around the room. Participants find, match and affix fabric shapes to the coat cut-out.
Storytelling 	Theme: We live together in families given to us by God. See Storytelling Script on the following page. Prepare Story Cards for Storytelling (Appendix I, pp. 117-119). Place the Bible and the Jesus doll with the Storyteller.

Exploring

Brown Bag Coats

For each participant, provide a brown grocery bag cut into a vest-type coat. Split the bag up the middle on the front side. Cut holes for arms at the sides. Create a neck hole in the "bottom" of the bag. Children decorate coats by gluing fabric scraps to the outside surface.

Family Collage

On 11" x 17" sheets of white paper, children create family collages using cut out pictures from magazines. Discuss the different individuals and families represented.

Bean-Family Matching Game

Participants sort various types of beans from one large mixed pile into like groups, identifying the similarities and differences.

Parachute Toss

Two or more participants and adults play together with a parachute or large sheet. Activities may include: tossing a beach ball or stuffed animal in the air and catching it, making a parachute mushroom. You may also choose to conduct other games or other group activities (Simon Says or Red Rover).

Regathering	Sing *He's Got the Whole World in His Hands*, focusing the verses on family members and those present (e.g. brothers/sisters, mothers/fathers, aunts/uncles, whole families). Singing *Jesu, Jesu* participants bring Eucharist elements to the Celebrant then sit in a circle around the Eucharistic table.

Eucharist

Sing: *Gather our Hearts*

Gather our hearts, oh God.
Gather our thoughts, oh God.
Bring us together around you.

Celebration of the Eucharist

Dismissal	All sing and sign *Jesus Loves Me*. Celebrant provides the blessing: Celebrant: "Go in Peace to Love and Serve the Lord." Participants: "Thanks be to God!"

Storytelling Script

Place the Bible and Jesus doll by the Storyteller.
Today's Storytelling uses the six Story Cards for this session found in Appendix I, pp. 117-119.

1. Joseph receives coat (November • Year 1 • 1 of 6)
2. Joseph thrown in pit (November • Year 1 • 2 of 6)
3. Joseph taken from pit (November • Year 1 • 3 of 6)
4. Joseph and guard (November • Year 1 • 4 of 6)
5. Joseph and brothers (November • Year 1 • 5 of 6)
6. Joseph hugs Jacob (November • Year 1 • 6 of 6)

Our story today is from our Bible (*show Bible*), our book that tells the stories of God and God's people, of Jesus (*show Jesus doll*), God's son, and of how much God loves us (*place hands over heart*).

Jacob was a man who had twelve sons, including the youngest two, Joseph and Benjamin. These last two brothers were very special in Jacob's life and got very special treatment from Jacob.

Joseph was not required to go out in the fields and work like the rest of the brothers. And, Joseph dreamed that he would be a very special person when he grew up. The brothers were angry about the way Joseph was treated and about his dreams. Even so, Jacob gave Joseph a very special coat with sleeves and patches of bright colors. *Show the first story card. Place it in view of the children.*

One day Jacob sent Joseph to find his brothers where they were at work. As Joseph approached them, the brothers could see Joseph's new coat and they became very angry. They ripped off his coat and threw him into a well. *Place the second story card next to the first.*

Then, the brothers decided to sell Joseph to some traders who were on their way to Egypt. Joseph was pulled from the well and given to the traders in exchange for money. *Show and place the third story card.* The brothers took Joseph's colorful coat home and told Jacob that Joseph must have been killed. Jacob was upset and so sad to have lost his son.

Joseph was taken to a country called Egypt and became the slave of the captain of the guard in a prison. But, he continued to be faithful to God and to pray and honor him everyday.

Eventually, Joseph became a very powerful and successful leader in Egypt. But, he always remembered his father and brothers, and missed them. *Show and place the fourth story card.* This was a time when water was scarce and food was hard to grow. Many people, including Joseph's family were hungry. Jacob sent his sons—all but Benjamin—to ask for help, not knowing that Joseph—his son—was a leader.

Joseph recognized them, but the brothers did not recognize Joseph! When they asked Joseph for help, Joseph told them to bring the youngest son, Benjamin (whom he missed very much), then he would help them. *Quietly, dramatically whisper:* It must have made his heart leap to know after all this time that his father and Benjamin were alive and well!

The brothers returned to Jacob, telling him of the leader's (Joseph's) request. Jacob was very sad to have to give up his second son, Benjamin. But there was no food to eat, something had to be done! Benjamin returned with the brothers to Joseph, the Egyptian leader. When Joseph saw his brother he was so happy! He began to cry and said to them all, "Do you not know me? Have I changed so much? I am your brother Joseph!" *Show and place the fifth story card.*

Joseph and Benjamin immediately hugged each other. Then, Joseph told them to go back and bring, Jacob to him.

As Jacob approached, Joseph ran to his father. They hugged each other and celebrated their togetherness! *Show and place the sixth story card.*

Amen.

After an appropriate pause, the Storyteller goes on to explain the activities of the day.

Rhythms of Grace • December Year 1

Theme: God knows me and is with me always.

Scripture: I praise you because I am wonderfully made (Psalm 139)

Date: _____

Location: _____

Volunteer Roles:

Facilitator _____

Storyteller _____

Celebrant _____

Center Leader _____

Guide _____

Items Needed for this Session

❑ **Gathering**
- ❑ paper doll people of various sizes and colors

❑ **Storytelling**
- ❑ Bible, Jesus doll
- ❑ Storytelling Script, Psalm Cards
- ❑ plastic eggs with small objects inside (1 per child)
- ❑ basket

❑ **Exploring**

Matching Game
- ❑ clip art images
- ❑ card stock
- ❑ scissors, glue

I Am
- ❑ simple people outlines made of construction paper
- ❑ poster board sheets (1 per child)

Mandalas
- ❑ sample of a basic mandala
- ❑ crayons, markers or colored pencils

What is it?
- ❑ brown paper lunch bags
- ❑ feathers
- ❑ small stones
- ❑ cotton balls
- ❑ beans, rice or grains

Creating with Play Dough
- ❑ play dough or modeling clay

❑ **Regathering**
- ❑ elements for the Eucharistic table (see Eucharist)

❑ **Eucharist**
- ❑ altar table and elements (pita bread, juice, chalice, paten, purificator, corporal, altar cloth)
- ❑ Bible and Jesus doll
- ❑ Eucharistic Prayer (see p.100)
- ❑ *Gather our Hearts* song lyrics (see p.99)

❑ **Dismissal**
- ❑ *Jesus Loves Me* song lyrics (see p.99)

❑ **Leaders and Aides Pre-service:** Set up space. Finalize details. Pray.
❑ **Leaders and Aides Post-service:** Clean-up and share feedback. Set dates, discuss theme for next month.

Rhythms of Grace

Today's Theme:	God knows me and is with me always.
Today's Scripture:	I praise you because I am wonderfully made (Psalm 139)

Our Worship Service

Gathering

Begin today's session by distinguishing paper dolls by size and color.

Storytelling

Today's story comes from the Psalms. Psalm 139 is about how wonderful God is.

Exploring

Matching Game
Play a familiar game to help discern how things are the same and how they are different.
(*communication*)

I Am
Explore and express what makes each of us unique with this poster craft activity.
(*fine motor, communication*)

Mandalas
Work with an ancient form to distinguish patterns.
(*communication, fine motor*)

What is it?
Use your sense of touch to perceive and identify objects hidden from view.
(*sensory integration, kinesthetic awareness, communication*)

Creating with Play Dough
Let your imagination guide your creativity in making objects from play dough.
(*fine motor, sensory integration, communication*)

Regathering

Become more aware of ourselves and of others with this guessing game.
Sing *Jesu, Jesu*.
We bring elements of the Eucharist to the Celebrant to create the Eucharistic table.

Eucharist

Sing: *Gather our Hearts*
Gather our hearts, oh God.
Gather our thoughts, oh God.
Bring us together around you.

Celebration of the Eucharist

Dismissal

Sing and Sign: *Jesus Loves Me*
Blessing
Celebrant: "Go in Peace to Love and Serve the Lord."
Participants: "Thanks be to God!"

This Month's Session Plan

Gathering

Before the session, cut paper doll people (approximately 3" x 5") from various colors of construction paper—multiple shapes per color. Spread people shapes on the floor of the worship space. Participants sort shapes by size and color while identifying and naming colors.

Storytelling

Theme: God knows me and is with me always.
Before the session, prepare plastic eggs with surprise contents and place in a basket. See Storytelling Script on the following page. Using Appendix I, p. 120, as a guide, create either individual verse cards, or a large Psalm 139 poster with all the listed verses and display prominently.
Place the Bible and the Jesus doll by the Storyteller.

Exploring

Matching Game

Before the session prepare paired flashcards using clip-art images and card stock. Create 10 or more pairs of cards. Participants play game of Concentration. Shuffle cards and arrange face down. Child flips two cards face up. Ask child to identify images, and to say if they match. If so, child retains the cards. If not turn the card back over. Vary the number of pairs used according to participant's ability.

I Am

Provide simple outlines of people made from construction paper. Mount the outlines on poster board (1 per child). Participants choose images about themselves (cut from magazines) around the outlines. Invite participants to tell why they chose certain images.

Mandalas

Before the session, find and print images of basic *mandalas* which have a distinct shape or shapes embedded within them. Explain that a *mandala* is a special circular image that is used to focus attention and to create a feeling of sacredness. Make copies (1 per participant) of one or more images. Provide crayons, markers or colored pencils. Invite participants to find the embedded shapes and color them.

What is it?

Before the session, place objects into individual paper bags. Participants place hands in bags, guessing the contents.

Creating with Play Dough

Provide play dough or modeling clay and a flat work surface. Participants create objects of their own choosing. Invite children to describe what they have made.

Regathering

Designate a leader. All participants gather in a circle with eyes closed. Leader chooses someone to leave the room. Once gone, those remaining open their eyes. The first to guess the missing person correctly becomes the new leader. Repeat as interest is maintained.
Singing *Jesu, Jesu* participants bring Eucharist elements to the Celebrant then sit in a circle around the Eucharistic table.

Eucharist

Sing: *Gather our Hearts*
Gather our hearts, oh God.
Gather our thoughts, oh God.
Bring us together around you.

Celebration of the Eucharist

Dismissal

All sing and sign *Jesus Loves Me*.
Celebrant provides the blessing:
Celebrant: "Go in Peace to Love and Serve the Lord."
Participants: "Thanks be to God!"

Storytelling Script

Place the Bible, Jesus doll and basket of plastic eggs by the Storyteller.
Post the Psalm 139 verses prominently in the worship space so you can refer to them during the Storytelling

Today, our story from the Bible—the stories of God's people and of his son Jesus—is not really a story. It is a *psalm*.

Many, many years ago, before Jesus was born, God's people were nomads. That means they moved from place to place and lived in very large tents. At night, God's people would sit around their fires and sing songs. These songs were taught to their children and their children's children.

Eventually the music was lost but the words were written down. These words are in a part of our Bible we call *the Psalms*.
Use the Bible to show the Psalms. Point out that each psalm has its own number.

This psalm, #139, (*point to all the Psalm Cards, or to Psalm 139 in your Bible*) talks about how wonderful God is.

This psalm also talks about how well God knows us.
Indicate and read from the V.1 Psalm Card. (Oh Lord, you have searched...)
God knows all about each one of us, God knows _____.

Share something that God knows about each person present.

Indicate and read the card with Verse 14. (I praise you because I am wonderfully made...)
Let's say those words together.
Repeat Verse 14.

I have in my hand an egg. I have a plastic one for each of you, too.
Pass around 1 egg for each person.

We know this is an egg because we know what they look like on the outside. But, we don't know what is inside. Just like real eggs, your eggs each have something inside, too, but we can't tell what it is without opening it up. It could be a hardboiled egg, an uncooked egg or a little chicken. We just don't know.
Pause, briefly.

We don't know, but God knows. God knows what we are like inside, too. God has known us since even before we were born!
Read Verse 14, again. (I praise you because I am wonderfully made...)

Our psalm also says that God always knows where we are, and if we try to hide from him—or if we get lost—he will find us.
Indicate and read the cards with Verses 1 (Oh Lord, you have searched...) and 3 (You see me, wherever I am...).

Let's all close our eyes and I will hide my egg.
Hide the egg somewhere in your worship space.

God knows where my egg is. Let's find it!
Participants look for the egg, and reform the circle after the egg is found.

Now let's guess what's in our eggs.
Invite each child to guess to their own ability. Then, open the eggs to discover what is hidden inside.

Conclude by reading V.14 again. (I praise you because I am wonderfully made...)

Amen.

After an appropriate pause, the Storyteller goes on to explain the activities of the day.

Rhythms of Grace • All Saints' • Year 1

Theme: We are all children of God, and saints in God's Kingdom.

Scripture: I John 3:1-3

Date: _____

Location: _____

Volunteer Roles:

Facilitator _____

Storyteller _____

Celebrant _____

Center Leader _____

Guide _____

Items Needed for this Session

❏ **Gathering**	❏ people pictures glued to white poster board circles, strung for hanging	❏ cloud shape made from foam core, ❏ paper clip hooks
❏ **Storytelling**	❏ Bible, Jesus doll ❏ Storytelling Script ❏ felt-board figures (male, female, adults and children—enough to represent all participants)	❏ gold or yellow felt halos to fit felt figures ❏ large felt heart shape ❏ picture of a saint with a halo ❏ picture of a stained glass window

❏ **Exploring**	**Balance Beam Walk** ❏ 2 or 3 wide flat boards, 12' total length	**Stained Glass Window Pictures** ❏ waxed paper ❏ colored tissue paper ❏ decoupage glue and paint brushes ❏ mat board frames to hold wax paper ❏ scotch tape
	Halo Ring Toss ❏ 1 dozen gold pipe cleaners formed into circles ❏ board with rows of cup hooks, 4" apart	
	Self Portraits ❏ white paper ❏ crayons, markers or colored pencils ❏ mirror(s) ❏ (*optional*) flesh-colored, head-shaped cut-outs	**Beaded Cross Necklace** ❏ assorted colors and sizes of beads ❏ string, clasps ❏ small crosses (1 per child)

❏ **Regathering**	❏ 26 cardboard rounds (12" dia.) with alphabet letters ❏ recorded music, player	❏ elements for the Eucharistic table (see Eucharist)
❏ **Eucharist**	❏ altar table and elements (pita bread, juice, chalice, paten, purificator, corporal, altar cloth) ❏ Bible and Jesus doll	❏ Eucharistic Prayer (see p. 100) ❏ *Gather our Hearts* song lyrics (see p. 99)
❏ **Dismissal**	❏ *Jesus Loves Me* song lyrics (see p. 99)	

❏ **Leaders and Aides Pre-service:** Set up space. Finalize details. Pray.

❏ **Leaders and Aides Post-service:** Clean-up and share feedback. Set dates, discuss theme for next month.

Rhythms of Grace

Today's Theme:	We are all children of God, and saints in God's Kingdom!
Today's Scripture:	I John 3:1-3

Our Worship Service

Gathering

Begin today's session by calling to mind and representing the "great cloud of witnesses"—the saints.

Storytelling

Today our story is about how each one of us is a child of God—a saint!

Exploring

Balance Beam Walk
Saints are people who help others. Experience the spirit of helping and of being helped.
(*kinesthetic awareness, communication, gross motor*)

Halo Ring Toss
Have fun with an old-fashioned game.
(*gross motor, kinesthetic awareness*)

Self Portraits
Create saint portraits that look just like you!
(*fine motor, kinesthetic awareness*)

Stained Glass Window Pictures
Explore the creativity of our sainthood with a colorful craft project.
(*fine motor, sensory integration*)

Beaded Cross Necklace
Make something to let others know what you know: You're a saint!
(*fine motor, sensory integration*)

Regathering

Play a letter recognition game that connects us to the Communion of Saints.
Sing *Jesu, Jesu.*
We bring elements of the Eucharist to the Celebrant to create the Eucharistic table.

Eucharist

Sing: *Gather our Hearts*
Gather our hearts, oh God.
Gather our thoughts, oh God.
Bring us together around you.

Celebration of the Eucharist

Dismissal

Sing and Sign: *Jesus Loves Me*
Blessing
Celebrant: "Go in Peace to Love and Serve the Lord."
Participants: "Thanks be to God!"

Session Plan: All Saints'

Gathering
Before the session, create people ornaments from magazine pictures of people glued to white poster board circles. Add a length of string and a paperclip hook. Hang large mat board or foam core "cloud" from the ceiling low enough so participants can reach the bottom of the cloud. Arriving participants choose ornaments and hang them from holes punched along bottom edge of cloud. Invite participants to talk about the photos.

Storytelling
Theme: We are all children of God, and saints in God's Kingdom!
See Storytelling Script on the following page.
Place the Bible, Jesus doll and pictures (stained glass window, saint) with the Storyteller. Use a felt board and figures to display groups of women, men, girls, boys, and a red felt heart to represent God. Participants show and talk about different examples of families.

Exploring

Balance Beam Walk
Create a simple balance beam by placing wide planks end-to-end at floor level (not elevated). Children work in pairs or with a guide to navigate the length of the balance beam with assistance. *Explain that a helping hand or shoulder to lean on can make all the difference!* Switch roles so all have a chance to help and be helped. Increase the level of challenge by closing eyes or moving backwards.

Halo Ring Toss
Before the session, mount hooks on board, 4" apart. Children toss pipe cleaner "halos", attempting to hook them onto the game board.

Self Portraits
Provide crayons, markers or colored pencils, paper. Supply mirrors in which children can study their own faces, then draw self-portraits. Highlight attention to detail (*hair color, eye color, freckles, etc.*) Help children identify and name facial features. Alternative: Provide flesh-colored head cut-outs (*ovals with ears*). Children draw-in facial features.

Stained Glass Window Pictures
Participants create stained glass windows by gluing small, random-shaped pieces of colored tissue paper onto waxed paper using decoupage glue. When dry, tape the windowpanes into mat-board frames, sized to fit.

Beaded Cross Necklace
Participants make beaded necklaces with crosses in the center. Children select small crosses and string the beads to make necklaces. Provide assistance as needed.

Regathering
Before the session, create a set of cardboard rounds (12" dia.) with alphabet letters on them (26 total). Lay out rounds in a large circle (not necessarily in alphabetical order.) Play lively music as participants move from round to round. When music stops, all freeze. Leader then chooses a saint's name from a leader's list. Participants name the first letter of the saint's name. The person on that letter steps inside the circle to become "a saint." Continue until all are in the circle. Finish by saying "We are all saints of God!" Singing *Jesu, Jesu* participants bring Eucharist elements to the Celebrant then sit in a circle around the Eucharistic table.

Eucharist

Sing: *Gather our Hearts*
Gather our hearts, oh God.
Gather our thoughts, oh God.
Bring us together around you.

Celebration of the Eucharist

Dismissal
All sing and sign *Jesus Loves Me*.
Celebrant provides the blessing:
Celebrant: "Go in Peace to Love and Serve the Lord."
Participants: "Thanks be to God!"

storytelling script

Place the Bible and Jesus doll by the Storyteller.
This story uses a felt board with an assortment of felt human figures to represent women, men, girls, boys, and also a red felt heart to represent God. You will also need a picture of a saint with a halo, and a picture of a stained glass window.

Our story today is from our Bible (*show Bible*), our book that tells the stories of God and God's people, of Jesus (*show Jesus doll*), God's son, and of how much God loves us (*place hands over heart*).

After Jesus had gone to live in heaven with God, his friends began to gather together and to pray and worship. They started the church. The church was like one big family. It was full of people who wanted to live like Jesus had taught them, and to worship God.

All of us come from families.
Share a description of your family, placing appropriate figures on the felt board. For example:
In my family, there is a mother, and a father, and two girl children and one boy child.
That is my family at home.

Who can tell me about their family at home?
Storyteller removes felt board figures and begins again, 'building' the family of one of the children. When several children have had a turn to build their felt board family, the Storyteller continues.

In the church, we believe that God is the head of our family.
We don't know what God looks like, but we do know that God is love. We will use this heart for God.
Place red heart at the top of the felt board.
One of Jesus' friends, John, believed that we are all members of God's family.

God's family is very, very, very big. Everybody in the church is in God's family. We are all children of God. Even the grown-ups are 'children' of God! I am a child of God.
Put a figure up on felt board to represent the Storyteller.

You (*child's name*) are a child of God.
Place a figure representing the child.
You (*name another child*) are a child of God
If children are able, they can place their own felt board figures. Continue until all children are represented on felt board. Leave figures in place on the felt board.

We are all members of God's family. We are all children of God.
The church calls us *saints*. All who follow God in the church are called saints.
Even those who have died and live now in heaven—they, too, are called saints.
We say that they watch over us. They are the 'great cloud of witnesses.'
Make an expansive gesture with your hands to suggest a great cloud.

Sometimes artists like to show that someone is a child of God,—a saint—by painting a golden halo over that person's head. *Show the picture of a saint with halo. Allow each child to add a felt halo to their felt figure.*

Sometimes we have pictures of saints in our colorful church windows.
Show picture of stained glass window.

Saints are people who love God and who show it by loving other people.

I am a saint. You (*child's name*) are a saint (*point to each child, repeat*).

We are all saints!

Amen.

After an appropriate pause, the Storyteller goes on to explain the activities of the day.

Rhythms of Grace • Nativity • Year 1

Theme: Jesus is born! We celebrate!

Scripture: The birth of Jesus
(Luke 1:26-38, 2:1-20)

Date: _____

Location: _____

Volunteer Roles:

Facilitator _____

Storyteller _____

Celebrant _____

Center Leader _____

Guide _____

Items Needed for this Session

❏ **Gathering**
- ❏ manger
- ❏ hay or straw bale
- ❏ rustic blanket (small)

❏ **Storytelling**
- ❏ nativity figures, wrapped and numbered (#1 Mary, #2 Gabriel, #3 Joseph, #4 stable, #5,#6,#7 cow, donkey, horse, #8 baby Jesus, #9,#10,#11 angels, #12-shepherds and sheep)
- ❏ Bible, Jesus doll
- ❏ Storytelling Script

❏ **Exploring**

Pomander Ornaments
- ❏ Clementine oranges
- ❏ small bowl of whole cloves
- ❏ green and red ribbon
- ❏ scissors

Sugar Cookie Stars
- ❏ cookie dough, flour
- ❏ rolling pin
- ❏ star-shaped cookie cutters
- ❏ yellow colored sugar
- ❏ cookie sheets
- ❏ sandwich bags
- ❏ an oven for baking

Pinecone Toss
- ❏ cinnamon scented pine cones from craft stores
- ❏ assorted baskets (large to small)

Baby Doll Swaddle
- ❏ doll babies
- ❏ rustic blankets, strips of muslin or burlap

Nativity Figure Straw Search
- ❏ durable nativity figures
- ❏ large Shredded Wheat® biscuits
- ❏ large plastic bin

❏ **Regathering**
- ❏ doll babies wrapped in blankets (1 per child)
- ❏ elements for the Eucharistic table (see Eucharist)

❏ **Eucharist**
- ❏ altar table and elements (pita bread, juice, chalice, paten, purificator, corporal, altar cloth)
- ❏ Bible and Jesus doll
- ❏ Eucharistic Prayer (see p. 100)
- ❏ *Gather our Hearts* song lyrics (see p. 99)

❏ **Dismissal**
- ❏ *Jesus Loves Me* song lyrics (see p. 99)

❏ **Leaders and Aides Pre-service:** Set up space. Finalize details. Pray.
❏ **Leaders and Aides Post-service:** Clean-up and share feedback. Set dates, discuss theme for next month.

Rhythms of Grace

Today's Theme:	Jesus is born! We celebrate!
Today's Scripture:	The birth of Jesus (Luke 1:26-38, 2:1-20)

Our Worship Service

Gathering

Begin today's celebration of the birth of Jesus by preparing a humble manger.

Storytelling

Today's story helps us to celebrate the story of Jesus' birth.

Exploring

Pomander Ornaments
Celebrate the birth of Jesus by making fragrant natural ornaments.
(*fine motor, sensory integration*)

Sugar Cookie Stars
Remember the Star of Bethlehem by making star shaped cookies.
(*fine motor, sensory integration*)

Pinecone Toss
Recall the spirit of Christmas and the Nativity with a fragrant pinecone game.
(*gross motor, kinesthetic awareness*)

Baby Doll Swaddle
Experience the comfort that baby Jesus felt being swaddled in a blanket.
(*sensory integration, kinesthetic awareness, fine motor*)

Nativity Figure Straw Search
Search for nativity figures and retell the nativity story.
(*sensory integration, communication, gross motor*)

Regathering

Recall the birth of Jesus with nurturing doll play, singing *Away in the Manger*.
Sing *Jesu, Jesu*.
We bring elements of the Eucharist to the Celebrant to create the Eucharistic table.

Eucharist

Sing: *Gather our Hearts*
Gather our hearts, oh God.
Gather our thoughts, oh God.
Bring us together around you.

Celebration of the Eucharist

Dismissal

Sing and Sign: *Jesus Loves Me*
Blessing
Celebrant: "Go in Peace to Love and Serve the Lord."
Participants: "Thanks be to God!"

Session Plan: Nativity

Gathering

Arriving participants help to prepare the manger for the baby, Jesus. Children pull straw from the bale, place it in the manger, top with a blanket and form a shallow space for the baby. Help children to become accustomed to the space as they move through it by placing hay bale and manger across the room from each other.

Storytelling

Theme: Jesus is born! We celebrate!

Before the session, make numbered gift tag labels from the template found in Appendix I, pp. 121-122. Wrap Nativity objects to create tagged packages to be opened during Storytelling. Place packages within reach of the Storyteller

See Storytelling Script on the following page.

Place the Bible and the Jesus doll by the Storyteller.

Exploring

Pomander Ornaments

Provide Clementine oranges (at least 1 per participant), whole cloves and ribbon segments. Participants push whole cloves into fruit randomly or in patterns to create fragrant ornaments. Tie with lengths of red and green ribbon to hang.

Sugar Cookie Stars

Provide cookie dough and star-shaped cutters. Dust tables with flour to prevent dough from sticking. Participants roll dough flat and cut out cookies to decorate with colored sugar and then bake. Prevent children from eating raw dough, and keep children at a safe distance from the oven. Pack baked cookies in sandwich bags to take home.

Pinecone Toss

Children to toss scented pinecones into baskets located 6'-8' away. A volunteer retrieves and returns thrown pinecones.

Baby Doll Swaddle

Provide an assortment of doll babies and rustic-blanket cloth. Demonstrate wrapping dolls in "swaddling clothes," to make them feel comfortable and secure. Some children might like to experience the sensation of being wrapped on their hands or arms.

Nativity Figure Straw Search

Provide several boxes of broken Shredded Wheat® biscuits in a large plastic bin. Bury Nativity figures in this "straw." Participants search for figures, identify them, and re-create the Nativity story, arranging figures in order of appearance.

Regathering

Provide children with baby dolls swaddled in blankets (1 per child). Participants sit in a circle holding and rocking the dolls. All join in quietly singing *Away in the Manger*.✳

Singing *Jesu, Jesu* participants bring Eucharist elements to the Celebrant then sit in a circle around the Eucharistic table.

Eucharist

Sing: *Gather our Hearts*

Gather our hearts, oh God.
Gather our thoughts, oh God.
Bring us together around you.

Celebration of the Eucharist

Dismissal

All sing and sign *Jesus Loves Me*.
Celebrant provides the blessing:
Celebrant: "Go in Peace to Love and Serve the Lord."
Participants: "Thanks be to God!".

> ✱ *Away In the Manger* is Hymn #101 in Hymnal 1982

Storytelling Script

Our story today is from our Bible (*show Bible*), our book that tells the stories of God and God's people, of Jesus (*show Jesus doll*), God's son, and of how much God loves us (*place hands over heart*).

This Jesus (*show Jesus doll*), is a grown-up Jesus. This Jesus taught us how to care for each other and showed us, by going to the cross, how much he loved us. This Jesus was a teacher. He healed sick people, fed the hungry and took care of the poor. But Jesus, just like all of us, started out as a baby.

Let's hear the story of how he was born.
I need helpers to tell the story.
Ask:
Who can be a helper?

Let me pass out these packages to you. Hold them in your laps until I ask for you to help me.
Distribute the wrapped, gift-tagged and numbered packages.

Begin with package #1. Ask:
Who has a package with #1 on it?
Can you open the package and show us what is in it?
Child opens #1 and finds figure of Mary.
Now, lets read what the gift tag says.
Read tag from package #1
Have child hold figure up for all to see and then place figure on the rug.

Continue in the same way with packages 2-9
Who has package #2,...?
Open the package and show what is in it...
Child opens the package and then its gift tag is read.
Child holds up package contents for all to see, then places it on the rug with the other objects, gradually assembling all the elements of the Nativity story.

Once the package containing the shepherds and the sheep (#9) has been opened, ask for the last three packages (#10, #11, #12) to be opened together. Read the Angel's gift tags in sequence.

Place angels, shepherd and sheep in the stable scene. Complete the telling of the story:

And so, the shepherds hurried to Bethlehem where they found Mary and Joseph and the baby Jesus, lying in a manger.

The shepherds knew that this was the beginning of something new and wonderful that God was doing. They knelt down and praised God. Then, they went out to tell everyone what God had done.

Amen.

After an appropriate pause, the Storyteller goes on to explain the activities of the day.

Rhythms of Grace • Epiphany • Year 1

Theme: The Good News of Jesus is made known to the world.

Scripture: The gifts of the Wise Men (Matthew 1:18–2:12)

Date: _____

Location: _____

Volunteer Roles:

Facilitator _____

Storyteller _____

Celebrant _____

Center Leader _____

Guide _____

Items Needed for this Session

❑ **Gathering**
- ❑ large star made from poster board

❑ **Storytelling**
- ❑ Bible, Jesus doll
- ❑ Storytelling Script, Story Cards
- ❑ large star from Gathering

❑ **Exploring**

Memory Strips
- ❑ long paper strips with 4 sections
- ❑ story cards (1 full set per child)
- ❑ glue
- ❑ crayons

Star Pictures
- ❑ star shapes made from yellow card stock
- ❑ crayons, markers or colored pencils
- ❑ glue
- ❑ decorative items
- ❑ magnets (1 per child) or string

Large Nativity Scene
- ❑ large examples of main figures (Mary, Joseph, Jesus, Shepherds, 3 Wise Men)
- ❑ outline of manger on the wall
- ❑ masking tape

Star Toss
- ❑ assorted containers
- ❑ star shapes made from colored household sponges

❑ **Regathering**
- ❑ elements for the Eucharistic table (see Eucharist)
- ❑ rhythm instruments

❑ **Eucharist**
- ❑ altar table and elements (pita bread, juice, chalice, paten, purificator, corporal, altar cloth)
- ❑ Bible and Jesus doll
- ❑ Eucharistic Prayer (see p. 100)
- ❑ *Gather our Hearts* song lyrics (see p. 99)

❑ **Dismissal**
- ❑ *Jesus Loves Me* song lyrics (see p. 99)

❑ **Leaders and Aides Pre-service:** Set up space. Finalize details. Pray.
❑ **Leaders and Aides Post-service:** Clean-up and share feedback. Set dates, discuss theme for next month.

Rhythms of Grace

Today's Theme: The Good News of Jesus is made known to the world.
Today's Scripture: The Gifts of the Wise Men (Matthew 1:18–2:12)

Our Worship Service

Gathering

Begin today's session by highlighting the stars in the sky.

Storytelling

Today's story is about the gifts of the three wise men, and the many gifts we can give to God.

Exploring

Memory Strips
Use today's Story Card images to create a take-home reminder of today's story.
(*fine motor, communication*)

Large Nativity Scene
Work together to form a large nativity mural on the wall of your worship space.
(*communication, gross motor, fine motor*)

Star Pictures
Create and share self-portraits that demonstrate we are all stars!
(*fine motor, communication*)

Star Toss
Recall today's story with a follow-the-star tossing game.
(*gross motor, kinesthetic awareness*)

Regathering

Sing *Joy to the World* to celebrate the new thing God has done.
We bring elements of the Eucharist to the Celebrant to create the Eucharistic table.

Eucharist

Sing: *Gather our Hearts*
Gather our hearts, oh God.
Gather our thoughts, oh God.
Bring us together around you.

Celebration of the Eucharist

Dismissal

Sing and Sign: *Jesus Loves Me*
Blessing
Celebrant: "Go in Peace to Love and Serve the Lord."
Participants: "Thanks be to God!"

Session Plan: Epiphany

Gathering	Create one large star (18"-24" dia.), from poster board or foam core. Provide a covered craft table and craft supplies. Before the session begins, make a plan to hang or display the completed star in the storytelling area. Participants work together to decorate the star.
Storytelling	Theme: The Good News of Jesus is made known to the world. Hang a large star made of poster board (see Gathering) on a wall or over the storytelling area. See Storytelling Script on the following page. Prepare Story Cards for Storytelling (Appendix I, pp. 123-124). Place the Bible and the Jesus doll by the Storyteller.

Exploring

Memory Strips

Before the session, make copies of the Story Cards for this session (1 set of copies per participant). Provide 2" wide paper strips long enough to accommodate all four cards in order. Divide strips into four sections. Participants glue story cards to strips in order as they retell the story.

Star Pictures

Cut out stars from yellow card stock. Participants draw a self-portrait on the star. Help participants write, "God's light shines here" around the portrait. Decorate and add a magnet on back or a hole for hanging.

Large Nativity Scene

Before the session, hang a large outline of a manger scene drawn on kraft or butcher paper on a wall. Create and cut out large card stock nativity-scene figures (the Holy Family, shepherds, angels, 3 wise men, etc.). Participants color these figures and place them on the wall in the scene outline while retelling the story. Invite children to name each figure as is placed.

Star Toss

Before the session, cut star shapes from assorted colors of clean, new household sponges. Participants toss stars into containers.

Regathering 	Provide rhythm instruments to use as accompaniment. Sing *Joy to the World* ✳ Singing *Jesu, Jesu* participants bring Eucharist elements to the Celebrant then sit in a circle around the Eucharistic table.
Eucharist	**Sing: *Gather our Hearts*** **Celebration of the Eucharist** Gather our hearts, oh God. Gather our thoughts, oh God. Bring us together around you.
Dismissal 	All sing and sign *Jesus Loves Me*. Celebrant provides the blessing: Celebrant: "Go in Peace to Love and Serve the Lord." Participants: "Thanks be to God!"

✳ *Joy to the World* is Hymn #100 in Hymnal 1982

Storytelling Script

Place the Bible and Jesus doll by the Storyteller. Place the large star made from poster board created in the Gathering activity above the head of the Storyteller.
Today's Storytelling uses the four Story Cards for this session found in Appendix I, pp. 123-124.
1. The Magi follow the star (Epiphany • Year 1 • 1 of 4)
2. The Magi approach Herod (Epiphany • Year 1 • 2 of 4)
3. The Magi present gifts (Epiphany • Year 1 • 3 of 4)
4. The Magi return home (Epiphany • Year 1 • 4 of 4)

Our story today is from our Bible (*show Bible*), our book that tells the stories of God and God's people, of Jesus (*show Jesus doll*), God's son, and of how much God loves us (*place hands over heart*).

Briefly recount the Nativity narrative, setting the stage for the Wise Men's visit:
Many years ago there was a young woman named Mary and a man named Joseph. An angel of the Lord went to Mary and then to Joseph to tell the good news: Mary was to have a baby!

Now, the country where they lived wanted to count all the people who lived there. Everybody was told to travel to where they were born. Mary and Joseph traveled to a place called Bethlehem.

When they got to Bethlehem there was no place for Mary and Joseph to stay. But, an innkeeper showed them an animal stable where they would be warm and protected. That night the baby Jesus was born.

Then describe the Wise Men's journey:
In the East (*indicate the eastern direction*) three Wise Men were following the special star in the sky. They had read that a very special "King" would be born, and that a special star would lead them to him.
Slowly make an arc with your hand from "pointing east", up to the large star hanging above the head of the Storyteller.

The Wise Men traveled many, many miles, and many, many days to find the special place, and the special child-the baby Jesus.
Show the first story card. Place the card in view of the children.

They asked the ruler of the land, a King named Herod, where they could find this "new King." *Show and place the second story card next to the first.*

The ruler was upset and confused. He knew of no "new King!" Herod asked the Wise Men to find this new King and tell him where he could be found so that he, too could honor him and worship him. This was a lie. Herod wanted to harm this new King and keep him from becoming the new ruler.

So, the Wise Men kept looking, and kept following the star.
Point to the first story card again.

They were amazed when they finally found the "new King"—the baby Jesus—in the stable with straw on the ground and the animals all around him. They each gave the child special gifts that would be given to a king: gold, frankincense (a perfume), and myrrh (a sweet smelling oil).
Show and place the third story card next to the second. Point to the various gifts.

Then the wise men left and returned home filled with wonder and joy.
Show and place the fourth story card next to the third. Indicate that the Wise men took a different path.

They did not tell Herod where to find the baby Jesus, and Jesus grew up in a loving family.

Amen.

After an appropriate pause, the Storyteller goes on to explain the activities of the day.

Rhythms of Grace • Holy Week/Easter • Year 1

Theme: Our journey with Jesus through suffering and coming to new life.

Scripture: The story of Easter (Matthew 21:1-9, 26:17–28:10, Mark 14:12–16:8, Luke 22:7–24: 12, John 18:1–20:18)

Date: _____

Location: _____

Volunteer Roles:

Facilitator _____

Storyteller _____

Celebrant _____

Center Leader _____

Guide _____

Items Needed for this Session

❑ **Gathering**
- ❑ *Hosanna/Alleluia* banners with words in "bubble letters"
- ❑ Crayons, markers or colored pencils
- ❑ tape for hanging banners

❑ **Storytelling**
- ❑ Bible, Jesus doll
- ❑ Storytelling Script, Story Cards

❑ **Exploring**

Preparing for the Last Supper
- ❑ Small table, chairs and tablecloth
- ❑ 13 plastic cups and plates
- ❑ place cards for Jesus and 12 disciples
- ❑ napkins (at least 1 per participant)
- ❑ pita bread, juice

Bread Dough Crosses
- ❑ pre-made bread dough
- ❑ flour
- ❑ non-stick cookie sheets
- ❑ sandwich bags
- ❑ an oven for baking

Foot Washing
- ❑ plastic basin
- ❑ pitcher of warm water
- ❑ towels

Garment Weaving
- ❑ fabric strips (2" x 12")
- ❑ construction paper (11" x 17"), with slits for weaving

❑ **Regathering**
- ❑ footprint cut-outs made from brown construction paper
- ❑ copies of Story Cards (1 set per family)
- ❑ (optional) palm leaves made of green construction paper, scroll or Bible, pita bread and juice, cross, large rock, basket of silk flowers
- ❑ elements for the Eucharistic table (see Eucharist)

❑ **Eucharist**
- ❑ altar table and elements (pita bread, juice, chalice, paten, purificator, corporal, altar cloth)
- ❑ Bible and Jesus doll
- ❑ Eucharistic Prayer (see p. 100)
- ❑ *Gather our Hearts* song lyrics (see p. 99)

❑ **Dismissal**
- ❑ *Jesus Loves Me* song lyrics (see p. 99)

❑ **Leaders and Aides Pre-service:** Set up space. Finalize details. Pray.
❑ **Leaders and Aides Post-service:** Clean-up and share feedback. Set dates, discuss theme for next month.

Rhythms of Grace

Today's Theme:	Our journey with Jesus through suffering and coming to new life.
Today's Scripture:	The story of Easter (Matthew 21:1-9, 26:17-28:10, Mark 14:12-16:8, Luke 22:7-24: 12, John 18:1-20:18)

Our Worship Service

Gathering

All are invited to help decorate the letters of the Hosanna/Alleluia banners.

Storytelling

Today's story tells of the great sacrifice that Jesus made for us and of God's amazing power.

Exploring

Preparing for the Last Supper
Become familiar with the Last Supper by setting the table and naming or counting those present.
(*gross motor, communication*)

Foot Washing
Learn one way that Jesus showed his friends that he loved them by the act of washing their feet.
(*sensory integration, fine motor, kinesthetic awareness*)

Bread Dough Crosses
Create an edible version of the symbol of the cross.
(*fine motor, sensory integration*)

Garment Weaving
Children practice the skills of simple weaving as a way to celebrate Jesus' triumphal entry into Jerusalem.
(*fine motor*).

Regathering

Learn about Jesus' Holy Week journey by walking the path and collecting a set of story cards to take home.
Sing *Jesu, Jesu*.
We bring elements of the Eucharist to the Celebrant to create the Eucharistic table.

Eucharist

Sing: *Gather our Hearts*
Gather our hearts, oh God.
Gather our thoughts, oh God.
Bring us together around you.

Celebration of the Eucharist

Dismissal

Sing and Sign: *Jesus Loves Me*
Blessing
Celebrant: "Go in Peace to Love and Serve the Lord."
Participants: "Thanks be to God!"

Session Plan: Holy Week/Easter

Gathering

Before the session create banner signs with the words *Alleluia* and *Hosanna* in large bubble letters. As participants arrive, invite them to color in the letters. These banners will be used during the Storytelling. Invite children to repeat the words Hosanna and Alleluia aloud as they are working.

Storytelling

Theme: Our journey with Jesus through suffering and coming to new life.
See Storytelling Script on the following page. Prepare Story Cards for Storytelling (Appendix I, pp. 125-127).
Place the Bible and the Jesus doll by the Storyteller.

Exploring

Preparing for the Last Supper

Set 13 places—plates, cups, and napkins—at the table. Use place cards to name places for Jesus and the 12 disciples. Invite children, as they are able, to read the names aloud or count the number of place cards. Compare and contrast meals that the participants have at home. Ask, "Is this meal anything like home?" "How so?"

Foot Washing

Using a basin, pitcher of water and towels, all take turns to washing each others' feet, or the feet of a doll.

Bread Dough Crosses

Roll strips of dough and press together into crosses. Place on cookie sheets sprayed with non-stick spray. Bake. Cool and place in bags to take home. Keep children from eating raw dough, and keep children at a safe distance from the oven.

Garment Weaving

Before the session, prepare large sheets of construction paper by cutting long horizontal slits in the paper at 2" intervals, and cut strips of remnant fabric. Participants weave 'garments' of paper and cloth to represent the cloaks that were strewn in Jesus' path at the Triumphal Entry.

Regathering

Using a large boot or shoe as a template, trace footprints on full sheets of brown construction paper. Cut out enough footprints to make a winding path with six stations. Make copies of full sets of today's story cards (1 per family). Separate the sets into stacks of like images. Place one stack at each station on the path. You may want to embellish each station with other related objects (palm frond, cup and plate, cross, rock that sealed the tomb, silk flower bouquet for Easter morning). As the children follow the path, a volunteer helps child to recall and describe the scene depicted. Children collect full sets of all six cards to take home for recalling the story with family and friends.
Singing *Jesu, Jesu* participants bring Eucharist elements to the Celebrant then sit in a circle around the Eucharistic table.

Eucharist

Sing: *Gather our Hearts*

Gather our hearts, oh God.
Gather our thoughts, oh God.
Bring us together around you.

Celebration of the Eucharist

Dismissal

All sing and sign *Jesus Loves Me*.
Celebrant provides the blessing:
Celebrant: "Go in Peace to Love and Serve the Lord."
Participants: "Thanks be to God!"

storytelling Script

Our story today is from our Bible (*show Bible*), our book that tells the stories of God and God's people, of Jesus (*show Jesus doll*), God's son, and of how much God loves us (*place hands over heart*).

This is a story that begins very happily, (*hold up Hosanna! sign, say 'Hosanna!' and have children repeat the acclamation*) and ends very, very happily (*hold up the Alleluia! sign, say 'Alleluia!' and have children repeat the acclamation*).

It is a very happy story at the beginning and at the ending, but has a very sad part in the middle. The story starts in Jerusalem. *Show the first story card. Place the card in view of the children.*

Jesus and his disciples came to the city to celebrate the Jewish festival of Passover, and the crowds were excited to see Jesus. Jesus was the man who had healed the sick and fed the poor and been a great teacher. And here he was!

The people celebrated by shouting "Hosanna!" (*Invite children to repeat "Hosanna."*) and by waving palm leaves from the palm trees. The people even put their coats on the ground so Jesus' donkey had a soft path to walk on!

When Jesus had arrived in the city, he shared a special dinner with his disciples. At this dinner they broke bread and shared wine. *Show and place the second story card next to the first.* Jesus showed his disciples that he loved them by washing their feet. He told his friends that he would not be with them much longer but that, after he was gone, they could always gather together for a meal just like this one and he would be with them again.

The disciples were sad that Jesus was going to leave them, and they were frightened.

After supper, Jesus and his friends went out to the Mount of Olives, to the garden of Gethsemane. *Show and place the third story card.*

Jesus went off, on his own, to pray. Jesus talked to God, his father. Jesus knew that his time to die was very close. And he prayed that God would be with him. The disciples did not understand. They were sad.

Soon, in the dark, soldiers came to arrest Jesus and took him away. Jesus was beaten and teased, and then he was nailed to a cross and left to die. *Show and place the fourth story card.*

Jesus had faith that this was what God had willed for him. And Jesus knew that, even as he died, God was with him.

Jesus' friends and his family were very, very sad. Jesus was dead, now. And he was buried in a cave with a giant stone rolled in front. A soldier was sent to guard the cave. *Show and place the fifth story card.*

Three days later, a miracle occurred. God's great power gave Jesus a new life! His friends went to see Jesus' dead body, and they found an empty grave! Jesus had risen from the dead! *Show and place the sixth story card.*

This was Good News. God was stronger than death. Jesus would live forever. The people shouted "Alleluia!" when they heard what God had done. *Invite children to repeat "Alleluia."*

Alleluia! Jesus is Risen!
The Lord is Risen, indeed! Alleluia!

Amen.

After an appropriate pause, the Storyteller goes on to explain the activities of the day.

Rhythms of Grace • Pentecost • Year 1

Theme: God's special gifts to all of his disciples—including us.

Scripture: Pentecost (Acts 2:1-21)

Date: _____

Location: _____

Volunteer Roles:

Facilitator _____

Storyteller _____

Celebrant _____

Center Leader _____

Guide _____

Items Needed for this Session

❑ **Gathering**
- ❑ straws
- ❑ ping-pong balls
- ❑ plastic buckets

❑ **Storytelling**
- ❑ Bible, Jesus doll
- ❑ Storytelling Script
- ❑ floor fan,
- ❑ party noise makers,
- ❑ poster board dove cut-out
- ❑ red and orange streamers

❑ **Exploring**

Pinwheels
- ❑ construction paper squares
- ❑ small flame and dove symbols (glue), or
- ❑ stickers with dove and flame images
- ❑ new pencils with full erasers
- ❑ small craft pins

Bubble Blowing
- ❑ bubble solution and wands for each participant
- ❑ drop cloth/floor protection

Water Table: Wind and Boats
- ❑ water table or large plastic bin, water
- ❑ plastic boats or other floating objects
- ❑ straws

Parachute or Sheet Toss
- ❑ parachute or large bed sheet
- ❑ beach ball or lightweight stuffed animals

❑ **Regathering**
- ❑ elements for the Eucharistic table (see Eucharist)

❑ **Eucharist**
- ❑ altar table and elements (pita bread, juice, chalice, paten, purificator, corporal, altar cloth)
- ❑ Bible and Jesus doll
- ❑ Eucharistic Prayer (see p. 100)
- ❑ *Gather our Hearts* song lyrics (see p. 99)

❑ **Dismissal**
- ❑ *Jesus Loves Me* song lyrics (see p. 99)

❑ **Leaders and Aides Pre-service:** Set up space. Finalize details. Pray.
❑ **Leaders and Aides Post-service:** Clean-up and share feedback. Set dates, discuss theme for next month.

Rhythms of Grace

Today's Theme:	God's special gifts to all of his disciples—including us.
Today's Scripture:	Pentecost (Acts 2:1-21)

Our Worship Service

Gathering

Begin today's Pentecost session by exploring the effects of wind.

Storytelling

Today's story tells of the coming of the Holy Spirit at Pentecost.

Exploring

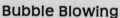

Pinwheels
Create a Pentecost Pinwheel to capture the wind.
(fine motor)

Bubble Blowing
Create bubbles and watch how the wind carries them.
(fine motor, gross motor, kinesthetic awareness

Water Table: Wind and Boats
Explore the power of wind to move objects and make waves.
(Sensory integration, communication)

Parachute or Sheet Toss
Experience the power of teamwork in parachute play.
(gross motor, kinesthetic awareness)

Regathering

Together sing *Ev'ry Time I Feel the Spirit*.
We bring elements of the Eucharist to the Celebrant to create the Eucharistic table..

Eucharist

Sing Gather our Hearts
Gather our hearts, oh God.
Gather our thoughts, oh God.
Bring us together around you.

Celebration of the Eucharist

Dismissal

Sing and Sign: *Jesus Loves Me*
Blessing
Celebrant: "Go in Peace to Love and Serve the Lord."
Participants: "Thanks be to God!"

Session Plan: Pentecost

Gathering

Provide ordinary drinking straws (1 per participant). Distribute ping-pong balls throughout the worship space. Place buckets on their sides as goals at various locations in the room. Participants blow air through straws to move ping-pong balls toward buckets or each other. Encourage children to simply have fun with the activity. Suggest pairing with a partner or working in teams or racing toward the goal bucket.

Storytelling

Theme: God's special gifts to all of his disciples—including us.

Before the session, position the electric fan, streamers and poster board cut-out of dove for use in Storytelling.

See Storytelling Script on the following page.

Place the Bible and the Jesus doll by the Storyteller.

Exploring

Pinwheels

Before the session, cut 6"-8" squares (1 per participant) from sturdy construction paper, fold on the diagonal, both ways. Cut along the folds from the corner to ½" from the center of the square. Provide stickers, stamps or cut-outs of Pentecost symbols (dove, flame). Participants decorate pinwheel form with symbols, then create their own working pinwheel by bending and pinning alternate corners of the form to the pencil eraser through the hole in the center.

Bubble Blowing

Provide plastic containers of bubble solution and bubble wands. Participants explore different ways to make bubbles, or play games (chasing, catching).

Water Table: Wind and Boats

In addition to the water table or large plastic bin with water, provide floating objects (boats) and straws for children to blow through. Participants explore the properties of floating objects and the effects of wind (breath). Play various games (boat races, obstacle course, explorer's journey, etc.) with the boats by guiding and steering them with the wind.

Parachute or Sheet Toss

Using a parachute or large bed sheet, participants toss and catch a beach ball or light-weight stuffed animal. Experiment with the effects that different motions have on the parachute (or sheet).

Regathering

Sing *Ev'ry Time I Feel the Spirit* ✱

Participants continue with this song while bringing Eucharist elements to the Celebrant then sit in a circle around the Eucharistic table.

Eucharist

Sing: *Gather our Hearts*

Gather our hearts, oh God.
Gather our thoughts, oh God.
Bring us together around you.

Celebration of the Eucharist

Dismissal

All sing and sign *Jesus Loves Me*.
Celebrant provides the blessing:
Celebrant: "Go in Peace to Love and Serve the Lord."
Participants: "Thanks be to God!"

 Ev'ry Time I Feel the Spirit is Hymn #75 in Wonder, Love and Praise.

storytelling script

Our story today is from our Bible (*show Bible*), our book that tells the stories of God and God's people, of Jesus (*show Jesus doll*), God's son, and of how much God loves us (*place hands over heart*).

Today's story is from the second part of our Bible, (*show Bible and divide in half*). The second part of our Bible is called the New Testament. It has the stories of Jesus and his followers. Today's story is about a special celebration we call Pentecost. Many people describe Pentecost as the birthday of the church. Our story from the New Testament will tell you why....
Recall and discuss the story of Easter, briefly.

After Jesus rose from the dead on Easter he spent time with his special followers, his disciples. But after 40 days Jesus told his friends it was time for him to go and be with his father, God.

He told the disciples that they were to continue his work here in the world. And he told them to teach others about how God wanted them to live and to love not only each other, but every living thing.

The disciples were afraid because they knew this would be a big job! How could they—just lowly humans—do this? Jesus told them, "You will receive power when the Holy Spirit has come upon you; and you will be my witnesses in Jerusalem, in all Judea and Samaria, and to the ends of the earth."

After he said this he rose up into the sky and was carried away to heaven.
Pause for a brief silence.

The disciples stood silently taking in all that Jesus had said and all that they had seen.

Ask:
How would you have felt after hearing and seeing all of this?
Allow children time to respond.

They went back to Jerusalem, to the room upstairs where they had stayed since Palm Sunday. There, they spent time in prayer and with each other, and the few others who had experienced the resurrection of Jesus.

Position an adult leader at the fan placed behind the participants and aimed at the dove and streamers. On the day of Pentecost the group was gathered together...

Begin, very dramatically...
All of a sudden there was a great rush of violent wind filling every room in the house!
Turn fan on, pointing at dove and streamers.

Flames of fire appeared and hung over their heads, but they were not hurt. The flame was the Holy Spirit and it filled them with gifts. These were the gifts Jesus had promised that the Holy Spirit would give them to help them continue Jesus' work here on earth.

So, these disciples were our first church because they continued to live, teach, and spread the story of Jesus and his life. They helped many people join Christian communities throughout the area. These communities, along with the disciples, continued living the lives that Jesus and God had intended for them.

These communities grew and became the first formal "churches" of the Christian faith—the family of God's people, where we all belong.

Amen.

After an appropriate pause, the Storyteller goes on to explain the activities of the day.

Rhythms of Grace • The Trinity • Year 1

Theme: The Mystery of Three-in-One, One-in-Three

Celebration: The Holy Trinity (Matthew 28:19-20)

Date: _____

Location: _____

Volunteer Roles:

Facilitator _____

Storyteller _____

Celebrant _____

Center Leader _____

Guide _____

Items Needed for this Session

❑ **Gathering**
- ❑ felt outline of person shape (3' x 2')
- ❑ corresponding felt cut-outs of body parts—hands (two), feet (two), arms (two), legs (two), full torso (one), head (one), hair (one)—made from different colors of felt
- ❑ felt board

❑ **Storytelling**
- ❑ Bible, Jesus doll
- ❑ Storytelling Script
- ❑ assembled felt figure from Gathering

❑ **Exploring**

Prayer Cube:
- ❑ pre-printed diagram of cube with prayers (see p. 129)
- ❑ crayons, markers or colored pencils
- ❑ clear adhesive tape
- ❑ 3" plastic photo cubes

Planting Seeds
- ❑ plastic pots and saucers
- ❑ potting soil, water
- ❑ clover seeds

Three-Part Puzzles
- ❑ assorted nature pictures mounted on card stock and cut into puzzle pieces (three pieces for each picture)

Trinity Symbol Stepping Stones
- ❑ 15-20, 8"-12" circles made from paper or foam sheets

❑ **Regathering**
- ❑ three hula hoops®, tape
- ❑ elements for the Eucharistic table (see Eucharist)

❑ **Eucharist**
- ❑ altar table and elements (pita bread, juice, chalice, paten, purificator, corporal, altar cloth)
- ❑ Bible and Jesus doll
- ❑ Eucharistic Prayer (see p. 100)
- ❑ *Gather our Hearts* song lyrics (see p. 99)

❑ **Dismissal**
- ❑ *Jesus Loves Me* song lyrics (see p. 99)

❑ **Leaders and Aides Pre-service:** Set up space. Finalize details. Pray.
❑ **Leaders and Aides Post-service:** Clean-up and share feedback. Set dates, discuss theme for next month.

Rhythms of Grace

Today's Theme:	**The Mystery of Three-in-One, One-in-Three!**
Today's Scripture:	**The Trinity (Matthew 28:19-20)**

Our Worship Service

Gathering

Begin today's Holy Trinity session by exploring the parts that make up the whole.

Storytelling

Today's story focuses on the Three-in-One mystery of The Trinity

Exploring

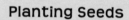

Prayer Cube
Create your own personal Prayer Cube with Grace prayers for use at home with meals. (*fine motor, communication*)

Planting Seeds
Plant clover seeds in pots for a growing reminder of today's three-in-one theme. (*sensory integration, fine motor, communication*)

Three-part puzzles
Explore today's three-in-one, one-in-three theme with puzzles made from nature scenes.
(*fine motor, communication*)

Trinity Symbol Stepping Stones
Use the symbol of the Holy Trinity as a way to create a path to follow.
(*kinesthetic awareness, gross motor, communication*)

Regathering

Get up and move around while exploring the symbol of The Trinity.
Sing *Jesu, Jesu.*
We bring elements of the Eucharist to the Celebrant to create the Eucharistic table.

Eucharist

Sing: *Gather our Hearts*
Gather our hearts, oh God.
Gather our thoughts, oh God.
Bring us together around you.

Celebration of the Eucharist

Dismissal

Sing and Sign: *Jesus Loves Me*
Blessing
Celebrant: "Go in Peace to Love and Serve the Lord."
Participants: "Thanks be to God!"

Session Plan: The Trinity

Gathering

Before the session, create from white felt a large (at least 3' x 2') cut-out in the shape of a person (similar in style to those in the transition icons, see left). In addition, make additional corresponding felt cut-outs of the hands (two), feet (two), arms (two), legs (two), full torso (one), head (one), and hair (one)—each from a distinct color of felt. Place the white felt outline on the felt board. The various felt parts are placed randomly around the room. As participants arrive, they locate the different felt parts. Each participant brings one (or more) parts to the felt board, identifies it, and places it on the white felt outline where it belongs. (Leave the "assembled" person together and in view of the storytelling area.)

Storytelling

Theme: The mystery of Three-in-One, One-in-Three!
See Storytelling Script on the following page.
Place the assembled figure from Gathering within view.
Place the Bible, the Jesus doll by the Storyteller.

Exploring

Prayer Cube

Provide prayer cube blanks (see p.129) (one per participant), crayons, markers or colored pencils, and 3" plastic photo cubes (1 per child). Participants add color to each prayer square or decorate as desired. Help children cut out each square and assemble the whole prayer cube to take home and use.

Planting Seeds

Provide small plastic pots and saucers (1 per participant), potting soil, and clover seeds. Participants plant several clover seeds under a thin layer of soil. Water thoroughly and let drain. Participants take pots home, continue to keep the soil moist and watch for 3-leafed clover to sprout, then recall today's three-in-one theme.

Three-Part Puzzles

Before the session, glue large rectangular pictures of nature scenes onto poster board. Cut each mounted picture into three puzzle pieces. Participants put pieces together and describe the resulting pictures. Make several puzzles and mix the pieces.

Trinity Symbol Stepping Stones

Before the session, make 15-20, 8"-12" circles from construction paper, poster board or foam. Distribute the circles in the room so that none of the edges are touching. Beginning at one side of the field of circles, participants gather three circles together overlapping edges to form a "trinity symbol stepping-stone." Create stepping stones in sequence to form a path across the field.

Regathering

Arrange the three hula hoops to form a Trinity Symbol (three intersecting/overlapping circles). Tape hoops in place. Participants step from one hoop into the next around the symbol repeating "Father, Son, and Holy Spirit." If ability allows, participants can *hop* or *jump* around the symbol rather than walk.
Singing *Jesu, Jesu* participants bring Eucharist elements to the Celebrant then sit in a circle around the Eucharistic table.

Eucharist

Sing: *Gather our Hearts*

Gather our hearts, oh God.
Gather our thoughts, oh God.
Bring us together around you.

Celebration of the Eucharist

Dismissal

All sing and sign *Jesus Loves Me*.
Celebrant provides the blessing:
Celebrant: "Go in Peace to Love and Serve the Lord."
Participants: "Thanks be to God!""

Storytelling Script

Our story today is from our Bible (*show Bible*), our book that tells the stories of God and God's people, of Jesus (*show Jesus doll*), God's son, and of how much God loves us (*place hands over heart*).

Today we will talk about *The Trinity*. The word *trinity* means three—as in "three of something."

At different times in the Bible the people of God thought of God in different ways. At times they thought of God as a *creator* and *protector*.

The Bible begins with God creating the world.

Later in the Bible—in the New Testament—when the people of God were part of Jesus' life or when they heard the stories of Jesus' life as we do, they believed that Jesus was the son of God. They thought of Jesus as a *teacher*, *healer* and *savior/redeemer*.

When Jesus rose into Heaven he told his followers that his Father, God, would send "another" in a different form. Those early Christians were to wait for this gift. Just a little while later God did send another—a helper—which came in the form of wind and flame. We call this part of God the Holy Spirit—*a power of God and life force* that gives each of us different gifts. Holy Spirit gives us what we need so we can live *with* God and *in* God and to tell others *about* God's amazing love.

> **The Father**
> Creator and protector
>
> **The Son**
> Teacher, Healer, Savior, Redeemer
>
> **The Holy Spirit**
> Power and life force

Refer to the felt person created for the Gathering activity

So God is like our person in the Gathering activity. God has three parts. Each part is and does a separate thing—just like each part of our body, is and does separate things.

We have hands that can clap (*everybody claps hands*) but our feet can't clap can they?

Our feet can kick (*stand and pretend to kick something*) but our hands can't kick.

Our hands and feet are separate parts that do different things. But, they are both part of your body!

The Trinity is like that. There are three separate parts, each with different abilities, but they are all part of God.

Three parts but one. One with three different parts.

Three in One, and One in Three. That's The Trinity.

Ask:
Now, how many parts did I talk about? Can anybody remember?
Invite answers.

Using the placard created for this session based on the text found in the box at the center of this page, review the different parts of God and what they each offer to our lives.

After an appropriate pause, the Storyteller goes on to explain the activities of the day.

Appendix I:

Rhythms of Grace • Year 1
Session Support Materials

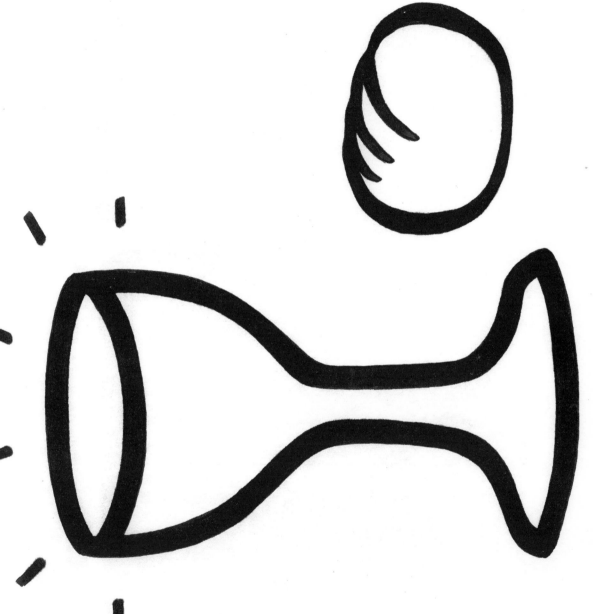

EUCHARIST

DISMISSAL

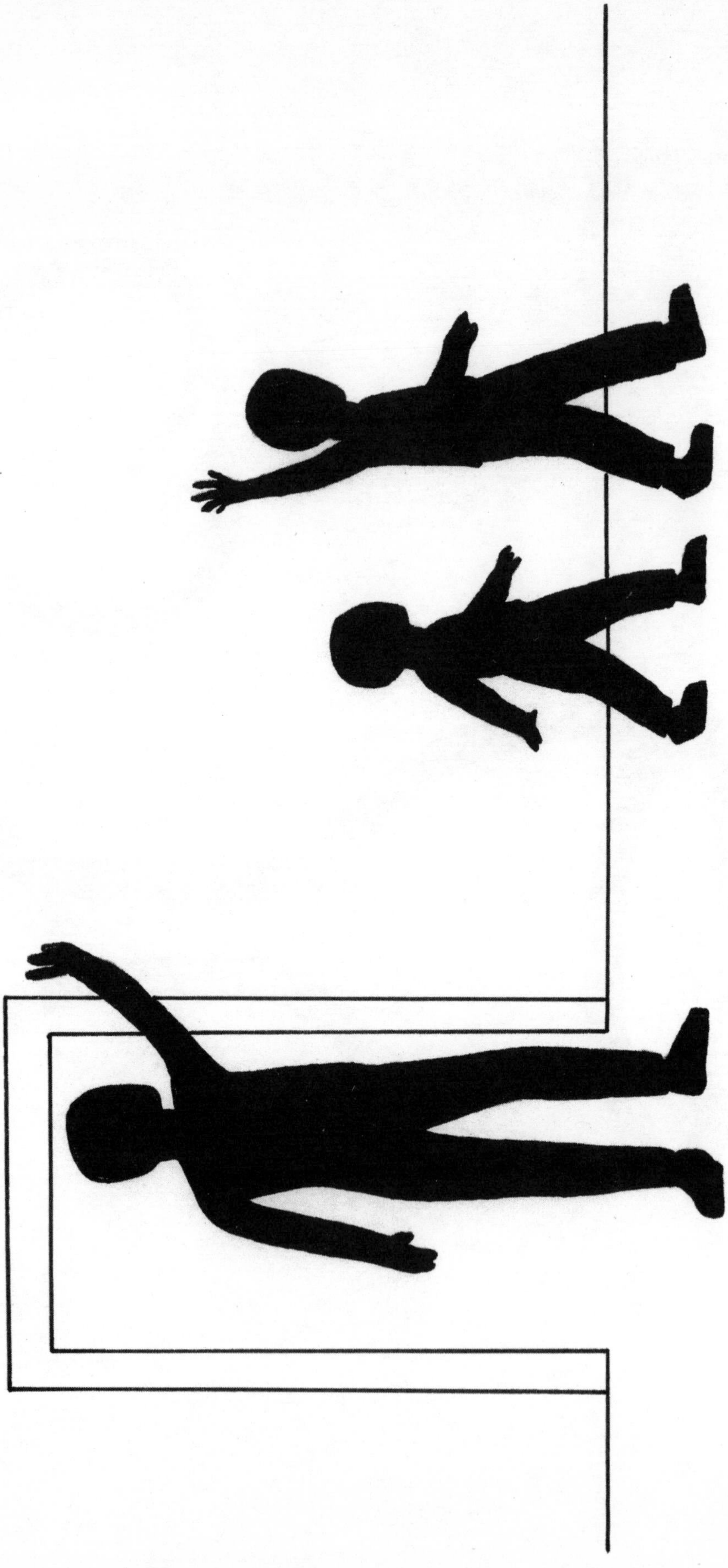

Gather Our Hearts

Ga - ther our hearts, O God, Ga - ther our thoughts, O God, Bring us to -

ge - ther a - round You!

Jesus Loves Me

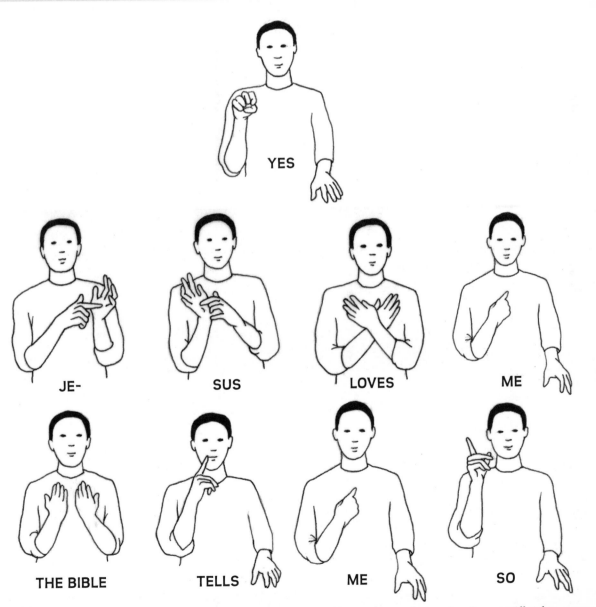

YES

JE-   SUS   LOVES   ME

THE BIBLE   TELLS   ME   SO

Eucharistic Prayer

(Celebrant may begin with the Sursum Corda)

Holy God,
We thank you for everything that you have given us:
This beautiful world,
Our families and friends,
Our gifts and abilities.

Especially, we thank you for sending us Jesus, your Son.
Jesus came and took care of the lonely and the sick,
the poor,
and the people who were left out.
And, he showed us how to love one another.

We learned, from Jesus to put you first, God, to love you, and to listen for your Word to us.
Jesus followed your Word and went to the cross, showing us that God's love could overcome even death, and bring new life.

For all this we thank you and praise you, saying:

> *Holy, holy, holy Lord,*
>
> *God of power and might,*
>
> *Heaven and earth are full of your glory,*
>
> *Hosanna in the highest.*
>
> *Blessed is the One who comes in the name of the Lord.*
>
> *Hosanna in the highest.*

On the night before he died, Jesus sat at the table with his friends. He gave them bread, and said, "Take and eat. This is my body, given for you." Then he took the cup, and gave it to them and said, "This is my blood. Whenever you drink it, I will be with you."

We now offer this bread, this wine- and ourselves- at this table in faith remembering that:

> *Christ has died.*
>
> *Christ is risen.*
>
> *Christ will come again.*

We ask that your Holy Spirit come to this table and fill this bread and this cup with God's powerful love that can make all things new. We pray that we, too, will be filled with the Spirit and joined together as one people blessed, and filled with hope.

We pray this, giving honor and praise to God: Father, Son and Holy Spirit.

> *Amen.*

And now, in the words that Jesus taught us we pray...

(Continue with Lord's Prayer, Fraction Anthem and Invitation to Communion)

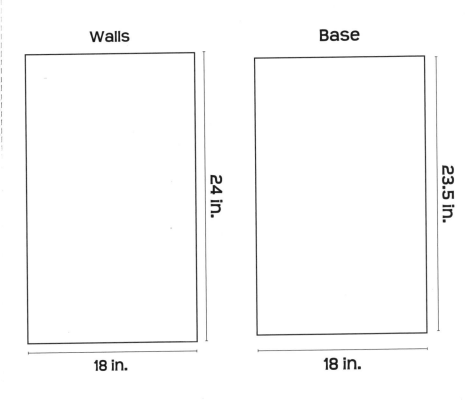

Walls

24 in.

18 in.

Base

23.5 in.

18 in.

Purchase sheets of foam core from a craft store or art supplies vendor.

Using the dimensional drawings at left as a guide, and a straight edge and a sharp craft knife, cut the various pieces from the foam core to the sizes indicated.

You will need two walls, one front, one back and one base. (Note: the Base dimension is slightly smaller on the long axis to accommodate the width of the two ends as the walls join the front and back sections. If your foam core is not ¼" thick, make adjustments to the length of the base accordingly to insure that the pieces fit correctly.)

Assemble the model and glue the walls together where the edges meet. You may want to reinforce the joints with tape to add structural strength. You may also want to create a stained glass window for the far end, and a hinged door for the front.

To make a stained glass window, sandwich pieces of colored tissue paper between two pieces of wax paper by pressing with a warm iron. Cut the resulting window to fit the arch-shape as indicated, Add cross pieces made from construction paper to form a cross in the window.

To form a hinged door, cut through the foam core along one whole side to the tip of the arch, then down the opposite side of the arch to the point where the edge straightens again. Leave the straight portion uncut, merely scoring through the inside surface creating a flexible hinge that allows the door to open outwards.

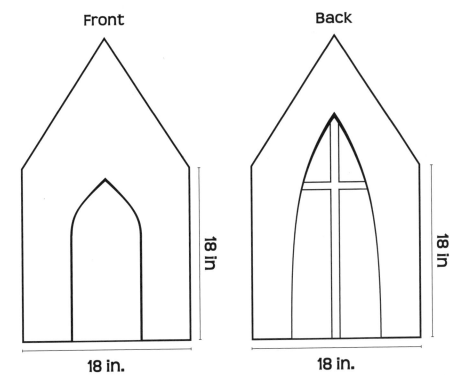

Front

18 in

18 in.

Back

18 in

18 in.

March • Year 1 • 1 of 3

March • Year 1 • 2 of 3

March • Year 1 • 3 of 3

Mary and the Gardener, John 20: 13-18 (additional reading: Matthew 28, Mark 16, Luke 24)
Display the Story Card among the items gathered for this story.

After Jesus died, his friends were very sad.

Just before dawn on the third day, Mary Magdalene and others went to the tomb. Imagine their surprise when they found that the big boulder had been rolled away from the opening. They looked inside and saw that Jesus' body was gone.

Then they saw a great white light—an angel, who told them that Jesus was alive. The others, Peter and John, ran back to the other disciples to tell them the news.

Mary walked slowly out of the tomb, thinking about what the angel had said. Could this be true? How? She started to cry. As she was crying and walking through the garden, she heard someone else. Was she not alone? Who could it be—the gardener?

She asked this person, "Do you know what has happened to Jesus? His body is gone. Do you know where they have taken him?" The person answered, "Mary!" Mary turned. The voice, it couldn't be. She looked again. It was! It was Jesus!

She fell to the ground crying tears of joy. She wanted to touch him for she couldn't believe her eyes.

Jesus told her, "Do not touch me now, but go and tell my other friends that I am alive!"

Mary ran all the way back, amazed!

Jesus was alive and she had seen him!

May • Year 1 • 1 of 3
© 2010 by Rhythms of Grace.

© 2010 by Rhythms of Grace.

May • Year 1 • 1 of 3

Road to Emmaus, Luke 24:13-33

Display the Story Card among the items gathered for this story.

On that same day, two of Jesus' friends were walking to the village called Emmaus just outside of Jerusalem.

They were still sad, but were talking about all that had happened. They were also a little confused after hearing what had happened to Mary earlier in the day.

While they were walking, a man came up to them and asked them what they were talking about. They said to him, "Have you not heard about the things that have taken place in the last few days?" They meant Jesus' death. They were sure everyone had heard about that!

The stranger said, "No. Tell me about that." So, they told him the story of Jesus' death, and then the story from the morning with Mary.

The stranger said to them, "Well, isn't this what the prophets foretold? How could you not believe it?"

And, they continued to walk and talk about all the things the prophets had said.

Toward the end of the day, as they came near Emmaus, it began to get dark. The two friends asked the stranger to stay with them for the evening.

When they sat down to eat dinner, the stranger took the bread, blessed it, broke it and gave it to them. All of a sudden they recognized him. It was Jesus!—but, then he vanished! Suddenly, they knew,

Jesus was alive and they had seen him!

May • Year 1 • 2 of 3
© 2010 by Rhythms of Grace.

May • Year 1 • 2 of 3

Fishing for Breakfast, John 21:1-14

Display the Story Card among the items gathered for this story.

A little while later, Jesus' friends were gathered by the shore of the Sea of Tiberias.

In the evening, one of the friends, Simon Peter told the others, "I am going fishing." All the others decided to join him, so they got into their boat and started out.

They fished with their nets all night long but at daybreak they had not caught a thing!

From the boat they could see a man standing on the beach. The man said to them, "You didn't catch any fish did you?"

The disciples said, "No."

Then, the stranger told them to throw their nets to the right side of the boat. They did as he said, and to their amazement the nets were now overflowing with fish.

At this point, they all realized that it was Jesus! Simon Peter jumped out of the boat and swam to shore.

As the boat came to the shore, all could see that there was a fire and fish cooking. Jesus said to them, "Come and have breakfast."

Jesus took the bread and gave it to them and did the same with the fish. They sat and had breakfast and talked.

Jesus' friends were so glad that

Jesus was alive and they had seen him!

May • Year 1 • 3 of 3
© 2010 by Rhythms of Grace.

© 2010 by Rhythms of Grace.

May • Year 1 • 3 of 3

Psalm 95

Come let us praise the Lord!

Let us sing for joy to God,

who protects us.

Let us come before him with thanksgiving

and sing joyful songs of praise.

For the Lord is a mighty God,

a mighty king over all the gods.

Psalm 95:1-3 (Good News Translation, Second Edition)

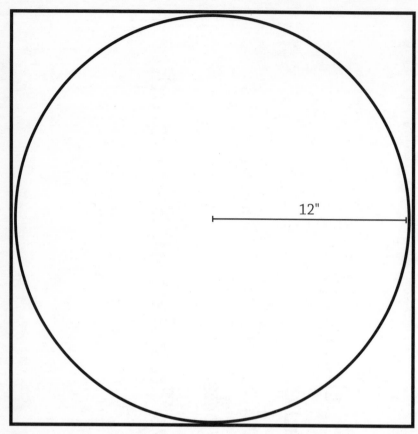

12"

To create the felt "world" for this session, begin with a 24" square of blue felt. Trace and cut out a 24" diameter circle.

Then, create the continents by scaling up the template drawing below, left. Using a 24" square piece of kraft or butcher paper, create a grid of lines, each 1½" apart, both vertically and horizontally.

Rather than drawing the continent figures "free hand," simply trace the pattern line that appears in each square until you have completed the outline of the desired continents.

Create a pattern by cutting out the continent shapes from the paper grid. Use brown or green felt.

You may choose to affix the continents to the blue background circle with fabric tape or fabric adhesive, or simply use them as you would other felt-board figures.

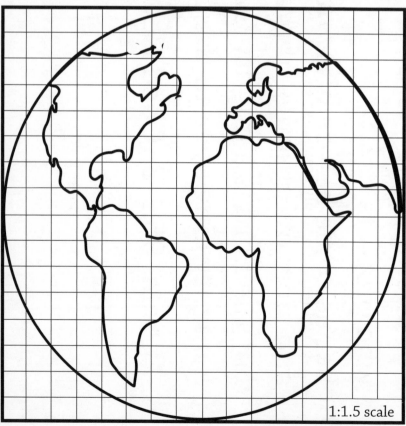

1:1.5 scale

THE LORD'S PRAYER IN COLORS : COLOR KEY

Our Father, who art in heaven, (white, the color of purity)

Hallowed be thy name. (yellow, the color of honor/majesty)

Thy kingdom come. Thy will be done, on earth as it is in heaven. (blue, the color of the sky)

Give us this day our daily bread, (brown, the color of wheat)

And forgive us our trespasses, as we forgive the trespasses of others. (red, the color of blood or wounds)

And lead us not into temptation, but deliver us from evil. (black, the color of darkness)

For thine is the kingdom, and the power, and the glory, forever and ever. (purple, the color of royalty)

Amen.

The Lord's Prayer

OUR FATHER

WHO ART
IN HEAVEN

HALLOWED BE
THY NAME

THY KINGDOM
COME

THY WILL
BE DONE

ON EARTH

AS IT IS
IN HEAVEN

GIVE US THIS DAY
OUR DAILY BREAD

AND FORGIVE
US OUR
TRESPASSES

AS WE FORGIVE THE
TRESPASSES OF
OTHERS

AND LEAD US NOT
INTO TEMPTATION

BUT DELIVER US
FROM EVIL

FOR THINE
IS THE
KINGDOM

AND THE
POWER

AND THE
GLORY

FOREVER
AND EVER,
AMEN.

October • Year 1 • 1 of 3

October • Year 1 • 2 of 3

© 2010 by Rhythms of Grace.

October • Year 1 • 3 of 3

November • Year 1 • 1 of 6

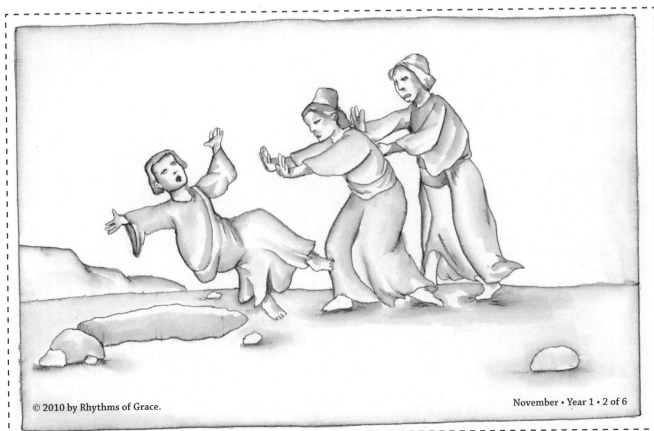

November • Year 1 • 2 of 6

November • Year 1 • 5 of 6

November • Year 1 • 6 of 6

Psalm 139

1. Lord, you have examined me and you know me.

2. You know everything I do; from far away you understand all my thoughts.

3. You see me, whether I am working or resting; you know all my actions.

4. Even before I speak, you already know what I will say.

5. You are all around me on every side; you protect me with your power.

6. Your knowledge of me is too deep; it is beyond my understanding.

7. Where could I go to escape from you? Where could I get away from your presence?

8. *(verse 8 omitted)*

9. If I flew away beyond the east or lived in the farthest place in the west,

10. you would be there to lead me, you would be there to help me.

11. I could ask the darkness to hide me or the light around me to turn into night,

12. but even darkness is not dark for you, and the night is as bright as the day. Darkness and light are the same to you.

13. You created every part of me; you put me together in my mother's womb.

14. I praise you because you are to be feared; all you do is strange and wonderful. I know it with all my heart.

(Good News Translation, Second Edition)

#1 Mary

Mary was a young woman who was picked by God to have a very special baby. The baby's name was Jesus.

#2 Gabriel

Gabriel was an angel sent by God to tell Mary that she would have a baby. At first Mary did not understand or believe the angel. But Mary prayed and said to God, "So be it with me, according to your word." That is how Mary said "Okay" to God.

#3 Joseph

Joseph was the husband of Mary. As the baby grew in Mary, it came time for Mary and her husband Joseph to go home to Joseph's hometown, Bethlehem. It was a long trip for Mary and Joseph. As they traveled, Joseph took good care of Mary and the baby growing inside of her.

#4 The Stable

When Mary and Joseph arrived in Bethlehem, they could not find a place to stay. It was late when they arrived and they were so very tired. Here is where Mary and Joseph spent the night—in a stable.

#5 A Cow

And in the stable there was a cow. All night long Mary and Joseph heard the cow making cow noises.

What noise does a cow make?

#6 A Donkey

And in the stable there was a donkey. All night long Mary and Joseph heard the donkey making donkey noises.

What noise does a donkey make?

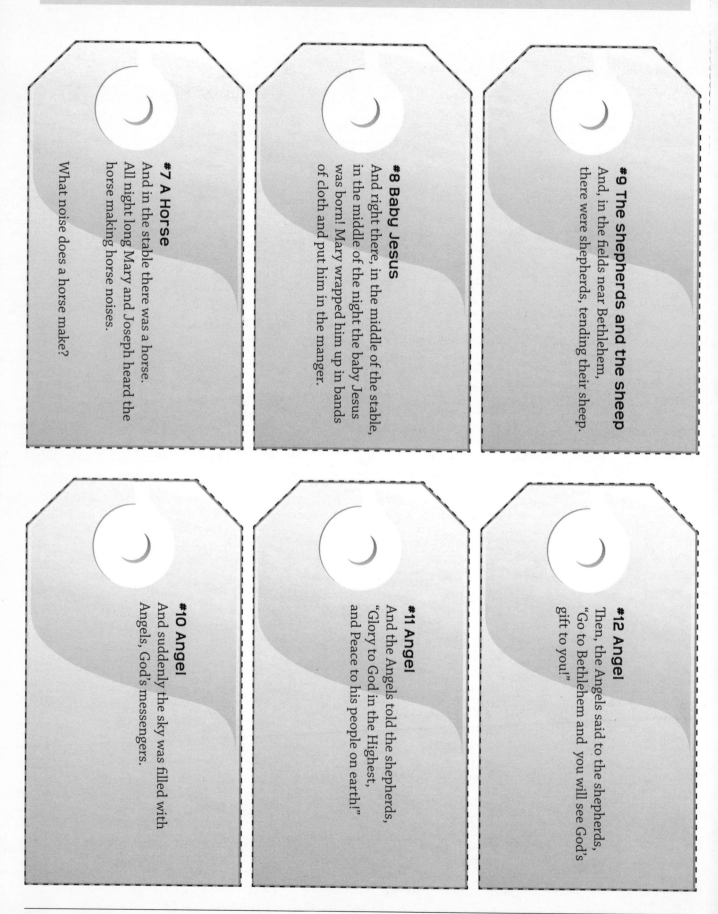

#9 The shepherds and the sheep
And, in the fields near Bethlehem, there were shepherds, tending their sheep.

#8 Baby Jesus
And right there, in the middle of the stable, in the middle of the night the baby Jesus was born! Mary wrapped him up in bands of cloth and put him in the manger.

#7 A Horse
And in the stable there was a horse. All night long Mary and Joseph heard the horse making horse noises.

What noise does a horse make?

#12 Angel
Then, the Angels said to the shepherds, "Go to Bethlehem and you will see God's gift to you!"

#11 Angel
And the Angels told the shepherds, "Glory to God in the Highest, and Peace to his people on earth!"

#10 Angel
And suddenly the sky was filled with Angels, God's messengers.

Epiphany • Year 1 • 1 of 4

Epiphany • Year 1 • 2 of 4

Epiphany • Year 1 • 3 of 4

Epiphany • Year 1 • 4 of 4

© 2010 by Rhythms of Grace.

Holy Week/Easter • Year 1 • 1 of 6

© 2010 by Rhythms of Grace.

Holy Week/Easter • Year 1 • 2 of 6

Holy Week/Easter • Year 1 • 3 of 6

Holy Week/Easter • Year 1 • 4 of 6

Holy Week/Easter • Year 1 • 5 of 6

Holy Week/Easter • Year 1 • 6 of 6

Oh, the Lord's been
good to me.
And so I thank the Lord,
for giving me
the things I need:
the sun and the rain
and the apple seed.
The Lord's been
good to me.

God is good
God is great
Let us thank Him
for our food.

In back of the bread
is the flour
In back of the flour
is the meal
In back of the meal
is the wind and the rain
and the Father's will.

Thank you God
for giving us food.
Thank you God
for giving us food.
For the friends we meet
And the food we eat.
Thank you God
for giving us food.

Thank you
for the world so sweet
Thank you
for the food we eat
Thank you
for the birds that sing
Thank you God
for everything.

Be present
at our table Lord
Be here
and everywhere adored.
From Thine own
bounteous hand our food,
May we receive
with gratitude.

Appendix II:
Resources for Implementing Rhythms of Grace

IMPLEMENTING RHYTHMS OF GRACE IN YOUR LOCAL SETTING

First Questions

Beginning a new program in any congregation or community of faith takes a considerable amount of prayer, planning, education, and coordination. Three questions should be addressed first in considering a new ministry:

- Is there a need, or 'market' for this program?
- Are there potential volunteers in the local church who will be invested in this ministry?
- Does this program have the support of the church leadership?

Determining the need for a ministry like *Rhythms of Grace* demands research outside the church community. Find and connect with local support groups for those challenged by the Autism Spectrum, those who have Down's Syndrome and other disabilities. Ask to come and talk about your idea at the group's regular meeting. Visit the school and speak to the elementary school principal or Special Education Chair about your desire to support families in their spiritual lives.

Sometimes civic officials can be wary of crossing church-state lines, but they may be willing to point you toward other support groups. Visit the local library and let the children's librarian know about your ideas. Send flyers to churches of all denominations in your area or ask to speak at a Clergy Association gathering. Is there a group of professional Christian Educators in your diocese or conference who might help to spread the word? Are there any particular families in your own congregation who might help to get the ball rolling?

Chances are, if you are reading this book, you have already identified a need in your ministry setting. Contacting others and sharing the news of your new program more broadly can only increase its success in ministering to a greater number of families.

Locating volunteers for a *Rhythms of Grace* program begins by knowing your congregation. Who are the teachers, nurses, social workers, Special Education professionals, artists and musicians in your church? Many of these people may already be committed to the regular church school program, but others who are not currently teaching may be intrigued by the nature of *Rhythms of Grace*.

Sometimes the *Rhythms of Grace* session is simply a better fit time-wise or represents a more attractive level of involvement for volunteers.

Initially, potential volunteers may express some reticence based on feelings of inadequacy or fear. "I wouldn't know how to help." "I'd be afraid I'd do something wrong." Educating the whole congregation about *Rhythms of Grace* and the population of children with special needs will help.

Get your clergy person on board. The approval of the local church leadership is vital in promoting any project. Educate your clergy and church council about the need for this ministry. Invite them to preach on the topic of hospitality, the Great Commission or the Baptismal Covenant in relation to *Rhythms of Grace*. Locate another church that has its own special needs ministry and call or visit with their pastor. Seeing a program in action can be the first step towards gaining support for one of your own.

"I love the crafts at Rhythms of Grace and how you help me. I have lots of fun, and I hope you do, too!"

Katherine, age 7

EDUCATING CHURCH MEMBERS

Because *Rhythms of Grace* is experiential in nature, one of the best ways to introduce the program to the congregation is by showing it to them. If your church has a coffee hour or fellowship time after worship, set up a table with two or three activities in which children and adults can engage. Some of the tactile activities are popular and fun: 'finger painting' with shaving cream on textured shelf paper, searching for Nativity figures in a bucket of straw, planting artificial flowers in a bed of potting soil. Put a card next to each activity that explains how it relates to a story from scripture and what therapeutic benefits it has for the participant.

Another way to educate members of the local church is by replacing one of the regular readings in worship with a Storytelling segment from *Rhythms of Grace*. Show the congregation how a story would be told at *Rhythms of Grace* using felt board or story boards or dramatic interpretation, and then explain its benefits to children and families with this particular set of needs.

Put inserts in your Sunday bulletin or newsletter about the prevalence of children with special needs in your community. Describe, briefly, some of the characteristics of these needs and ways that they can be accommodated. Using the appropriate language to describe exceptional learners can be a vocabulary lesson for many members of the congregation who may be accustomed to outdated terms.

Give concrete suggestions in a small booklet to local church members about how to engage individuals with special needs, such as allowing for a longer 'wait time' when asking questions, or using fewer words when making conversation or giving clear, concise directions. By doing this, you are empowering your congregation and eliminating some of the fear and reticence.

Invite a parent of a child with special needs in your congregation to talk about their experience with their children and the challenges that they face in daily life. Encourage the parent to also share the joys of their family life. Ministry to and with special needs children and their families must be seen as a celebration of life and not an opportunity for pitying.

> "Rhythms of Grace is a nice place to have reunions with God and family and friends."
> Alex, age 16

SUGGESTIONS FOR HOW TO ENGAGE WITH A CHILD WITH AUTISM

Communication

- *Simple directions.* Use as few words as possible, speak slowly and give 3 steps or less in a sequence.
- *Enough response time.* When asking questions or giving directions give child ample time to respond.
- *Eye contact.* Do not force eye contact for a child with autism.
- *Repetition.* Ask child to repeat key words in directions to verify understanding.
- *Pictures.* Use visual cues whenever possible to accompany verbal directions.
- *Listening.* Never assume that a child with autism is not listening, even if they appear to be "in their own world."

Schedules

- *Transitions.* Give warnings, use visual cues (icons or signs), use auditory cues
- *Routine.* Keep to same routine when possible. If a variation is expected, give ample warning. Review routine at the beginning of the day, breaking it down into small chunks. Give visual guides to remind child of the schedule.
- *Advance notice.* Give a 'count down' ("5 minutes," "3 minutes," "1 minute") when it is time to change activities.
- *Auditory cues.* Use music to aid in transitions. Sing a song as activities change, or use a bell or recorded music as a cue.

Physical

- *Firm touch.* Firm, consistent pressure is best. Soft, soothing 'back rubs' or 'reassuring' arm brushing or tapping can be unsettling.
- *Firm brushing.* Use a firm stroking motion in one direction on arms or legs for soothing.
- *Gross-motor precedes fine-motor.* Jumping, running or swinging arms vigorously can help to settle a child for fine-motor activities.
- *Avoid loud noises.* Prepare child when possible for loud noises. Allow children to cover ears or leave area.
- *Limit self-stimulating.* Set limits on 'stimming' (lights, waving fingers, patterns) time.
- *Sensory defensiveness.* Notice and plan for particular likes/dislikes. Note which textures are unsettling for some and soothing for others.

Social

- *Safe place retreat.* Provide safe space from which to observe—allow child to retreat to safe space with comfort objects if activity becomes overwhelming.
- *Buddy pairs.* Support, encourage and facilitate friendship and pairing.
- *Use a timer.* Set limits for conversation about one topic.
- *Words and deeds.* Use a verbal description to match a physical/social cue. For example, say, "I am happy to see you" with a smiling face.

THE CHARACTERISTICS OF AUTISM AND CHRISTIAN PEDAGOGY

Rhythms of Grace is a worship and formation experience that is designed to suit all learning types. It is intentional in offering storytelling methods and exploration activities to suit a variety of learning styles and modalities. That, in itself, is good pedagogy. It is understood that we all have different learning preferences and the best teachers and curricula offer multiple means of introducing and exploring different concepts.

Jesus knew this and used parables and 'object lessons' to teach his disciples. Think of Jesus drawing the little child into his lap and saying "to such as these belong the Kingdom of God..." (Matthew 19:14), or his Feeding of the Multitudes, or the cursing of the fig tree. These object lessons made his point where mere words or explanations would not have been as clear or as well received.

Most of the children who worship with us at *Rhythms of Grace* can be described as "on the Autism Spectrum." Following is a list of the most typical characteristics of autism. Because autism is a spectrum disorder, not all children will exhibit all of these characteristics, and each characteristic will be expressed in varying degrees, depending on the individual.

In general, autism affects the development of social interaction and communication, can involve sensory sensitivity, and can include the presence of stereotyped behavior.

Children with autism may express these characteristics:
- inability to read social cues
- inability to understand body language
- sensitivity to loud noises
- sensitivity to particular textures
- sensitivity to textures, colors, aromas, particularly in food
- sensitivity to light
- fixation on one particular area of interest
- difficulty with transitions
- incessant need for conversation on one topic with no regard for social exchange
- self-stimulating behavior or "stimming" (flicking fingers, blinking eyes, shaking hands, rocking, gazing at lights or ceiling fans in motion)
- self-injurious behavior when excited (biting hand)
- inability to make or keep eye contact
- toe walking
- delay in, or lack of, spoken language development
- receptive language difficulty
- monotone speaking voice
- echolalia (repeating words of another)
- scripting (repeating dialogue from movies or TV programs)
- difficulty moving body through space
- poor kinesthetic awareness

VOLUNTEER RECRUITMENT

Once the program has been introduced to the parish and the clergy or leadership has voiced its support, the next step is to invite volunteers. Some may have come forward during the education phase and expressed an interest, others may have watched from the fringes, observing carefully before making a commitment. Go through the membership roster and make note of those who have shown an active interest so far. Go through the list again and make a list of those who may not have asked for information, but who may have a gift or talent that would benefit the *Rhythms of Grace*.

Call everyone on the first list and invite them to an informational meeting. Call everyone on the second list and invite them to the same meeting, but tell them why you think they would be a good addition to the *Rhythms* team: "Mary, I know that you play guitar, would you be willing to consider *Rhythms of Grace* as a place to share that gift once a month?" "Joe, your talent in drawing might be just what we need to help us design felt board figures for our new special needs ministry. Would you be willing to come to a meeting to learn more about it?" By naming the individual's gift, their starting place in the program is defined and their comfort level is increased.

Specific gifts or highly developed talents are not required to serve on a *Rhythms of Grace* team. Sometimes something as simple as a nimble frame or youthful age is enough: "Fred: we need someone who can get down and crawl around on the rug when we do an obstacle course for the kids." "Lauren, a few teenagers helping at *Rhythms* would really help, small children need older role models. Can you come and bring a friend?"

Getting prospective volunteers to the first meeting and then to the first *Rhythms of Grace* session are the two biggest hurdles. Reducing the potential volunteer's anxiety by identifying other participants helps a great deal. As the 'yes' list for the organizational meeting grows, identify this group to each other: "Joe, Mary said that she would come to our first *Rhythms* meeting. Fred and Lauren are coming, too. Can you join us? I think you'd make a great addition to the group."

When verbal commitments have been made, send out a reminder to the group that more fully explains the agenda of the informational meeting.

> "Surely, God is in this place."
> Harriet, teen volunteer

RHYTHMS OF GRACE INFORMATIONAL MEETING

> Come and See!
> Rhythms of Grace
> a ministry to and with special needs children and their families
> invites you to an Informational Meeting
> On (date) at (Place)
> From (time) – (time)
> Come and learn how you can share the Love of God in
> Play-do and prayers, crafts and communion.
>
> We will hear about the program and
> see a demonstration of a
> Rhythms of Grace Bible Story
> &
> Craft Activity.
>
> For more information… call XXX- XXXX

At this informational meeting, the following should be offered:

- Prayer-in thanksgiving for individual gifts, in thanksgiving for open and inquiring hearts, for families who face challenges with joy, for the love of Jesus
- A theological grounding of *Rhythms of Grace* as a response to Jesus' call to care for those on the fringes of our communities and a fulfillment of our (Episcopal) Baptismal Covenant including the theological idea of *Rhythms of Grace* as its own unique expression of the Body of Christ
- A description of the *Rhythms of Grace* format and flow (Gathering, Storytelling, Exploring, Re-gathering, Holy Eucharist, Dismissal)
- A discussion of various special needs populations and the ways that a *Rhythms* program accommodates them
- A sample Story and Exploring activity (select from any session plan)
- A description of the Volunteer Roles
- A discussion of time commitment
- A review of Child Safety policies, practices and procedures in place to adhere to—including routine background checks
- A time for Questions and Answers
- A place sign up for Volunteer Training, indicating any area of special interests or talent.(ie: I would like to play guitar… I like to do crafts, etc.)

The role of the facilitator of this meeting is to be hospitable, making everyone feel comfortable, and to be cogent. A listening heart will sense those who need extra support or more information, and will encourage those whose enthusiasm is a sign of the Spirit, blessing this new venture.

VOLUNTEER TRAINING

There are three components of volunteer training for *Rhythms of Grace*: a mandatory training session where hands-on experience is gained, the completion of all necessary diocesan/provincial paperwork to insure safe-church policies and procedures are followed, and the commissioning of new volunteers in the regular worship setting.

Prayer

Open the training session with a prayer that invites the Holy Spirit into the space to inspire and excite the group, to calm nervous hearts, to lift up the needy and to seek Jesus' presence in the group.

Give thanks for the gathered people of God.

Introductions

Invite each member of the group to introduce themselves and to offer what drew them to this new ministry, and what their hopes and dreams are for the program and their participation in it.

Role Description

Review the volunteer roles with all assembled. Encourage the individuals to consider where they see themselves fitting in, but to hold an open mind as to how they might function in all of the roles described.

Show & Tell

The best way to train for *Rhythms of Grace* is to move through a *Rhythms* service, imagining that the other participants are present. This gives the volunteers a sense of the flow and space of the program so that they will be familiar with the format when the actual participants arrive. Before the volunteer trainees arrive, set up the room as it would be for a *Rhythms of Grace* service. Prepare a Gathering activity, Storytelling session, Exploration Activities and a Regathering game. Assemble the elements for Communion. Walk the trainees through a service allowing the volunteers to participate in the activities as though they were the children.

Questions and Answers

Invite the volunteer trainees to reflect on the model service and how it felt to them. Respond to any questions or concerns. Ask if they can see themselves leading activities, songs, storytelling and games.

Additional Reading Material

Have on display a variety of resources that the volunteer trainees can peruse and borrow. There are many resources available on-line or copy and distribute the special needs bibliography (Appendix II, p. 143-144) for further study.

Sign up sheet

Encourage volunteer trainees to sign up for one or more *Rhythms of Grace* sessions noting their participation as Storyteller, Guide, Center Leader or Facilitator.

Make note on the sign up sheet which lesson plans will be used on which date. Distribute copies of specific session plans to each volunteer who has signed up for a particular session.

Commissioning

In the Episcopal Church, the appropriate validation of a new ministry in the church takes place in the context of a liturgical celebration. *The Book of Occasional Services* (BOS) provides a context for the commissioning of new ministries such as *Rhythms of Grace*.

The form for Catechist or Teachers (#5) or Other Lay Ministries (# 16) is most appropriate. The Commissioning takes place following the sermon at the Eucharist. There is a brief Examination that notes that each of us is called by God and equipped with special gifts, and a presentation of the candidates for ministry. It is recommended that this celebration take place annually, as new volunteers are added to the *Rhythms of Grace* community. (Feel free to adapt the process of Commissioning according to your own denomination's accepted practices.)

PUBLICITY: WHO

An Ecumenical Effort

Rhythms of Grace is intended as an ecumenical program that welcomes participants from all Christian traditions. In practice this means that all mainline Christian liturgical denominations can adapt the basics of *Rhythms of Grace* to the principles and practices of their own faith heritage and their own faith tradition to create a "new thing" appropriate to their own context. An ecumenical focus also means that even within a particular faith tradition we recognize that there still is room to welcome others from other traditions for the sake of sharing our Christian values in the context of a supportive community. Finally, the ecumenical nature of *Rhythms of Grace* means that communities of worship might form and grow simply as communities of co-worshipping Christian families with special needs—only loosely associated with an identified base church or home denomination. What is most important in each case is simply that an opportunity is created for those in need to come together, hear the word of God and celebrate the gifts of the Eucharist in an atmosphere of welcome, support and comfort.

Notice of the local *Rhythms of Grace* program should be broadcast through all the local churches—in their newsletters, on their Websites, and in their Sunday bulletins. It may be initially difficult to get another church to post the events of a neighboring parish in their own newsletters, but if an effort is made by the *Rhythms of Grace* minister to speak at different community gatherings in town, this can happen as the relationship grows, the need is recognized, and a level of trust is established.

Taking Pictures, Protecting Privacy

A note about pictures: It is true that one picture is worth a million words, especially in the publicity business. But any time that photographs are used, it is important to gain permission in writing to post the pictures.

PUBLICITY: WHAT

Getting the Word Out

The easiest, and most obvious, place to begin publicity for a new *Rhythms of Grace* program is in the host congregation. Even when the proper groundwork is laid, following the schedules of the Christian education program and getting the leadership on-board, it is still necessary to talk about the program, show posters about the program, make announcements about the program and include bulletin inserts and flyers about the program in the Sunday leaflets. Even then, it can be guaranteed that someone, hours before the first session begins will say: "*Rhythms of Grace*... what's that?"

Studies have shown that it takes most people a minimum of eight exposures to a new idea or event before they are likely to remember it or have it register in their brains. This is especially true in active parishes where myriad ministries are being conducted. In publicizing *Rhythms of Grace* in your church, be sure to use multiple venues and remember the multiple learning styles that people possess: use print materials as well as verbal announcements. Try to enlist a variety of voices to help talk about your program. After a time, even the most dynamic preacher's voice falls on deaf ears, if that is all the congregation hears. Invite the new volunteers to speak in front of the church. Invite a participating parent to mention at announcement time how exciting they find the new program. Put flyers on tables in the church hall, make note of the program in the newsletter, post colorful signs in the corridors and rest rooms of the parish house.

Begin publicity early and keep it fresh! Post pictures from the most recent *Rhythms* session on the bulletin board and include a notice of upcoming events: "Our next meeting is on (date)... Join us as we hear the story of (scripture and theme) and make (mention craft item here) All Are Welcome!"

PUBLICITY: WHERE

In Town

Local communities have many places in which to advertise a new program that ministers to special needs children and their parents: grocery stores, libraries (especially children's sections), town recreation areas, day cares, gyms, laundromats, post offices, delis, coffee shops and other places that children and parents frequent are ideal. Other opportunities for local publicity include doctor and dentist offices, veterinarians, dance and karate studios. Few of these places would consider a special church service as 'competition,' but some may have restrictions about what is allowed in their particular venue. Be sure to ask before posting any flyer or brochure. Public primary, intermediate and middle schools are other possibilities once official clearance has been obtained from the local Board of Education.

The Special Needs Network

Most special needs groups have a lively internet support system that includes Web sites, message boards and blogs. There are local support groups for parents with children of all sorts of needs that meet in homes, schools and at community colleges. Search for these groups online or ask at a regional social services office. Once a connection with a parent support group is made, the word about *Rhythms of Grace* will spread quickly.

Another opportunity for publicity exists at popular road races or other fund-raising events that benefit various special-needs groups. Many of these races and events sponsor fairs adjacent to the event. A *Rhythms of Grace* booth that features some hands-on activities will serve as a good draw and give a chance for conversation. Recreation Fairs are also held regionally and vendors of all sorts set up booths. *Rhythms of Grace* is appropriately included in these fairs and, because of the religious nature of the program, vendor fees may be waived.

Establishing an Internet Presence

An internet presence is important in promoting any activities or events in the 21st century. At a minimum, *Rhythms of Grace* should be listed as a ministry on the host church Web site, but a separate Web site or social media Web presence is also something to consider.

Many potential regular participants will search for *Rhythms of Grace* after hearing about it in a secular setting. A separate site that offers general information, specific scheduling details and directions is helpful. (Visit www.rhythms-of-grace.org to see how we've constructed our own Web site.)

Many support networks will happily list *Rhythms of Grace* on their Web sites as links, too. Take advantage of the network and outreach power of online social media. Link with friends, fans and other supporters in your local area and connect with those across the country involved in similar endeavors.

Raising Needed Funds

Grant funds are available for programs like *Rhythms of Grace*. Investigate the local diocese for program or mission development grants, other cooperating churches whose conferences might have funding, special needs support groups, or large churches in the United States who have money set aside to fund missions in smaller parishes.

In the early days of *Rhythms of Grace*, no collection was taken at the service. We considered *Rhythms* to be an outreach ministry of the parish. Soon, families who came to *Rhythms of Grace* from outside the parish wanted to make contributions as a way to say thank you for the service and to support its ongoing life as a ministry to the community. We now put an offering plate out near the door and many families elect to support the program with regular contributions.

FUNDING NEEDS AND PRIORITIES

A *Rhythms of Grace* program can be started with a few essential items that are inexpensive and easy to find. As time goes on and the program develops, and as storage space allows, additional materials can be purchased. Many of the supplies used in a typical *Rhythms of Grace* program are already part of a church school supply inventory, or can be found at home. Funding to begin a program should include:

Room furnishings and program basics:
- Jesus doll
- Tables and chairs for adults and children
- 9' x 12' rug for storytelling if area is not carpeted
- Large pillows or beanbags for storytelling area
- 3' x 4' felt board and yards of felt to create figures
- Plastic tubs and storage crates

Basic craft supplies:
- markers, paint, crayons, scissors, construction paper, glue, glue sticks, foam squares, beads, string, yarn
- Bean bags, playground ball, large laundry-type wicker basket
- Small table for altar
- Yard goods for altar cloth

Other helpful items:
- CD Player
- Music stand
- Small trampoline
- Stuffed animals for Safe Area
- Rocking chair
- Full length mirror (shatterproof)

Most of these items are already found in even modestly equipped church schools and, if the staff is willing to share, a *Rhythms of Grace* program can begin with very few additional materials.

Publicity costs:
- Flyers and/or brochures to introduce the program
- Posters
- Possible newspaper advertisement
- Establishing and maintaining a Web site

Staffing:
Quality staffing is essential. Will the *Rhythms of Grace* minister be a new, paid position, or will it be filled by a current staff member (clergy or Director of Religious Education) or will it be staffed wholly on a volunteer basis? The time needed to recruit and train volunteers, publicize the program, prepare lessons and acquire supplies is significant. The role of the *Rhythms of Grace* minister is vital to the program's success.

BIBLIOGRAPHY

Books about Children and Autism

Cohen, Shirley. *Targeting Autism*. Berkeley, CA: University of California Press, 1998.

Notbohm, Ellen. *Ten Things Every Child With Autism Wishes You Knew*. Arlington, TX: New Horizons, Inc., 2005.

Powers, Michael D., Psy.D. *Children with Autism: A Parent's Guide*. Bethesda, MD: Woodbine Houe, 2000.

Simmons, Karen L., ed. *Official Autism 101 Manual*. Alberta, Canada: Autism Today, 2006.

Ellen Notbahm and Veronica Zysk. *1001 Great Ideas for Teaching & Raising Children with Autisms of Asperger's*. Arlington, TX: Future Horizons, Inc. 2004, 2010.

Lears, Laura. *Ian's Walk: A Story about Autism*. Morton Grove, IL: Albert Whitman and Co., 1998.

Experience with the Disabled/Memoir

Grandin, Temple. *The Way I See It: A Personal Look at Autism and Asperger's*. Arlington, TX: Future Horizons, 2008.

Grandin, Temple. *Thinking in Pictures. My Life with Autism*. New York: Vintage Books, a division of Random House, 1995, 2006.

Grandin, Dr. Temple and Sean Barron. *Rules of Social Relationships: Decoding Social mysteries through the Unique Perspectives of Autism*. Arlington, TX: Future Horizons, Inc., 2005.

Haddon, Mark. *The Curious Incident of the Dog in the Night-Time*. New York: Vintage Books, a division of Random House Inc., 2004.

Nouwen, Henri J.M. *Adam: God's Beloved*. Maryknoll, NY: Orbis Books, 1997.

Stacey, Patricia. *The Boy Who Loved Windows* Cambridge, MA: Da Capo Press, 2003.

Church and Christian Formation

Breeding, MaLea, Dana Hood, Jerry Whitworth. *Let All the Children Come to Me*. Colorado Springs, CO: Cook Communications Ministries, 2006.

Kutz-Mellem, Sharon. *Different Members, One Body*. Louisville, KY: Witherspoon Press, 1998.

Newman, Barbara. *Autism and Your Church*. Grand Rapids, MI: Faith Alive Christian Resources, 2006.

Newman, Gene and Tada, Joni Eareckson. *All God's Children: Ministry with Disabled Persons*. Grand Rapids, MI: Zondervan, 1993.

Rapada, Amy. *The Special Needs Ministry Handbook: A Church's Guide to Reaching Children with Disabilities and their Families*. Amazon/BookSurge Publishing, 2007.

Webb-Mitchell, Brett. *Unexpected Guests at God's Banquet: Welcoming People with Disabilities into the Church*. New York: Crossroad, 1994.

BIBLIOGRAPHY (CONTINUED)

Theology

Bishop, Marilyn E., ed. *Religion and Disability: Essays in Scripture, Theology and Ethics*. Kansas City, MO: Sheed & Ward, 1995.

Block, Jennie Weiss. *Copious Hosting: A Theology of Access for People with Disabilities*. New York: Continuum, 2002.

Eiesland, Nancy L. and Don E. Saliers, eds. *Human Disability and the Service of God: Reassessing Religious Practice*. Nashville, TN: Abingdon Press, 1998.

Foley, Edward, ed. *Developmental Disabilities and Sacramental Access*. Collegeville, MN: The Liturgical Press, 1994.

Reynolds, Thomas E. *Vulnerable Communion: A Theology of Disability and Hospitality*. Grand Rapids, MI: Brazos Press, 2008.

Vanier, Jean. *Encountering the Other*. New York: Paulist Press, 2005.

Children's Bibles

Henley, Karyn, compiler. *The Beginner's Bible*. Grand Rapids, MI: Gold'n'Honey Books, Questar publishers, Inc., 1989.

Hastings, Selina, retold. *The Children's Illustrated Bible*. New York: Dorling Kindersley Book, 2000.

Lloyd-Jones, Sally. *The Storybook Bible: Every Story Whispers His Name*. Grand Rapids, MI: Zondervan, 2007.